HOLY SPIRIT AND HIS ROLE

AS SEEN IN THE BIBLE

LESLIE M JOHN

HOLY SPIRIT AND HIS ROLE

AS SEEN IN THE BIBLE

LESLIE M JOHN

DESCRIPTION

Holy Spirit is the third person of the Triune God – God the Father, God the Son and God the Holy Spirit. They are not three Gods, but they are three in One. Their roles as seen in the Bible are different from each other. They all work for common goal.

Inasmuch as the Holy Spirit is the living person, we do not refer Him as "it", but we refer Holy Spirit as "Him".

"But when the Comforter is come, whom I will send unto you from the Father, even the Spirit of truth, which proceedeth from the Father, he shall testify of me" (John 15:26)

Holy Spirit convicts of

- SIN

- RIGHTEOUSNESS
- JUDGMENT

This book deals with the specifics of the functions of the Holy Spirit, and His role in the Godhead, as seen in the Bible.

ABOUT THE AUTHOR

The author, who accepted Lord Jesus Christ as his personal Savior when he was a boy of 13, was raised in a Christian family and had education in Christian Institutions.

This then was the message that he heard of the Son of God, Lord Jesus Christ. This then is the message that he declares that God is light and in Him there is no darkness at all. Jesus Christ is the Son of God sent from above to save sinners.

Jesus died on the cross bearing our sins upon Himself. He was buried and God raised Him on the third day. Jesus, after having appeared to many for 40 days ascended to heaven. He will come again. Whosoever confesses his/her sins to Him and believe in heart that God raised Him from the dead will not perish but will have everlasting life.

"Jesus saith unto him, I am the way, the truth, and the life: no man cometh unto the Father, but by me" (John 14:6).

SCRIPTURES

Scriptures quoted in this book are from KJV from open domain, and from NIV, ESV, and NLT not greater than the number permitted.

Holy Bible, New International Version®, NIV® Copyright ©1973, 1978, 1984, 2011 by Biblica, Inc. ® Used by permission. All rights reserved worldwide.

The Holy Bible, English Standard Version. ESV® Permanent Text
Edition® (2016). Copyright © 2001 by Crossway Bibles, a
publishing ministry of Good News Publishers.

ISBN 13:   978-0-9985181-4-5
ISBN 10:   0-9985181-4-X

Table of Contents

CHAPTER 1

WHO IS HOLY SPIRIT?

"Nevertheless I tell you the truth; it is expedient for you that I go away: for if I go not away, the Comforter will not come unto you; but if I depart, I will send him unto you. And when he is come, he will reprove the world of sin, and of righteousness, and of judgment: Of sin, because they believe not on me; Of righteousness, because I go to my Father, and ye see me no more; Of judgment, because the prince of this world is judged" (John 16:7-11)

Inasmuch as the Holy Spirit is the living person, we do not refer Him as "it", but we refer Holy Spirit as "Him".

"But when the Comforter is come, whom I will send unto you from the Father, even the Spirit of truth, which proceedeth from the Father, he shall testify of me" (John 15:26)

Holy Spirit convicts of

- SIN
- RIGHTEOUSNESS
- JUDGMENT

THE SPIRIT OF LORD JESUS CHRIST

Lord Jesus Christ said after He has gone to the Father, Holy Spirit will come into this world and will help His disciples with teaching of all things and bringing to our remembrance all that He said to them. The disciples did not understand, until after His resurrection from the dead, many things the Lord said to them while He was on this earth calling for repentance, performing miracles, and healing the sick etc.

After forty days of His staying in this world after resurrection in order to show Himself that He has risen from the dead, the Lord ascended into heaven. He is now seated at the right hand of the Father and pleading on our behalf. While the Lord is in heaven, His Spirit is in our hearts guiding us, comforting us, teaching us the things of God.

Holy Spirit is living person, and, therefore, we do not refer Holy Spirit as "it", but we refer Holy Spirit as "Him". While the Lord Jesus Christ is pleading on our behalf with the Father all the time, His Spirit is in us comforting us, and guiding us.

"Consequently, he is able to save to the uttermost those who draw near to God through him, since he always lives to make intercession for them" – Hebrews 7:25 ESV

"If then you have been raised with Christ, seek the things that are above, where Christ is, seated at the right hand of God" – Colossians 3:1 ESV

The Lord said He will be with us forever providing us heavenly peace, the peace that transcends every understanding. His Spirit is always with us and is in us.

God is Triune; the Father, the Son, and the Holy Spirit. They are not three Gods, but One God in three. Their functions are different, yet they are one.

Anyone understanding Holy Spirit as a different entity other than the Spirit of Lord Jesus Christ, gets into trouble of misunderstanding and misinterpreting Scriptures. Those, who misunderstand Scriptures and misinterpreting them go further accusing Christians, who do not behave in a peculiar way of worshipping that they do not have Holy Spirit in them.

When an unbeliever accepts Lord Jesus Christ as his/her savior, He instantly comes into his/her heart. That is to say His Spirit instantly enters and lives in his/her heart.

"For God so loved the world, that he gave his only Son, that whoever believes in him should not perish but have eternal life" – John 3:16 ESV

"Have this mind among yourselves, which is yours in Christ Jesus, who, though he was in the form of God, did not count equality with God a thing to be grasped, but emptied himself, by taking the form of a servant, being born in the likeness of men. And being found in human form, he humbled himself by becoming obedient to the point of death, even death on a cross. Therefore God has highly exalted him and bestowed on him the name that is above every name, so that at the name of Jesus every knee should bow, in heaven and on earth and under the earth, and every tongue confess that Jesus Christ is Lord, to the glory of God the Father" – Philippians 2:5-11 ESV

"But the Helper, the Holy Spirit, whom the Father will send in my name, he will teach you all things and bring to your remembrance all that I have said to you" – John 14:26 ESV

We are sealed with the Promise of the Holy Spirit after we have heard the word of truth, the Gospel of salvation, and believed in Lord Jesus Christ, who gave His Spirit in our hearts as a guarantee. He said, "…I will never leave you nor forsake you." – (cf. 2 Corinthians 1:22; Ephesians 1:13; Hebrews 13:5 ESV)

Holy Spirit never enters the heart of an unbeliever. However, He starts convicting unbeliever as soon as the unbeliever starts responding to the preaching of the Gospel. Thus, He reproves him/her of sin, and of righteousness and of judgment. God gave apostles, prophets, evangelists, pastors and teachers to preach, teach the Word of God, and baptize those who accept Lord Jesus Christ as their personal savior (Ephesians 4:11).

Immediately an unbeliever accepts Jesus as Lord and confesses his/her sins to the Lord, and believes in heart that God raised Him from the dead on the third day, he/she is saved and assured of everlasting life, and sealed with the earnest of the Spirit in their hearts (cf. 2 Corinthians 1:22).

Does Holy Spirit do the work directly, independently, secretly – NO! The conversion is always by preaching, and the listener hearing the word, and by believing in the Word of God. Holy Spirit by means of WORD convicts, paves the way for conversion, and indwells heart.

"So then faith cometh by hearing, and hearing by the word of God" (Romans 10:17)

The Lord opens the heart through the preaching of the Gospel. Those who hear the Word of God, believe and obey. When you hear the Gospel of Jesus Christ, it pricks the heart. Holy Spirit shows you the Truth. That is how Holy Spirit convicts of sin, righteousness, and judgment. He does not do anything by stealth, or independently and never directly. Holy Spirit never convicts anyone of sin, righteousness, and judgment where there is no preaching done, or some reading material relating to Gospel of Jesus Christ is not provided.

Once, Holy Spirit indwells the heart of the saved one, the action is irreversible. It is immediate and it is God's act. The believer in Christ does not need to wait for Holy Spirit to indwell him/her. The indwelling of Holy Spirit is not an action by man, but is it the act of God.

 "Now when they heard this, they were pricked in their heart, and said unto Peter and to the rest of the apostles, Men and brethren, what shall we do?" (Acts 2:37)

Acts 16:14-15 – Paul preached. Lydia heard the Gospel of Jesus Christ and believed in Jesus Christ.

Acts 18:1-8 – Paul preached, Crispus believed and obeyed the WORD of God.

There are many more examples.

CHAPTER 2

REPROVING THE WORLD - OF SIN

In John 15:18-27 Lord Jesus speaks saying the world hated Him because the world did not and does not know that He came from the Father and they do not, therefore, believe in Him. Comforting the disciples the Lord says that inasmuch as the world hated Him, it is beyond any doubt that the world hates His disciples, as well.

The world persecuted Lord Jesus, and therefore, it is sure that they will persecute His disciples, as well. If the Lord did not incarnate and descended into this world and spoken the truth, they would not have been guilty of sin, but because He revealed the truth they are guilty of sin. They have no excuse now saying they never heard the truth. They hated the Lord Jesus and the Father. They hated the Lord without any cause.

It is this reason why the Lord said that when He goes to the Father, He will send a helper who proceeds from the Father and bears witness of Lord Jesus Christ. Inasmuch as the disciples were with Him, He said they would also bear witness of Lord Jesus Christ.

Based on the command the Lord gave in Matthew 28:19-20, all the followers of Lord Jesus Christ are His disciples in the present age. The disciples were commanded to go into the world, teaching all nations, baptizing them in the name of the Father, and of The Son, and of the Holy Spirit. We, as believers in the Lord, having heard the word, and saved by faith in Lord Jesus Christ, are now His disciples.

The finished works of Lord Jesus Christ were enough to save us from perishing unto eternal life. It is by confession that Jesus is Lord, and by believing in heart that God raised Him from the dead, we are saved (c., Romans 10:9-10). Our faith in the Lord Jesus Christ has made us His disciples.

REPROVING OF SIN

Lord Jesus Christ said, when the Holy Spirit comes into this world, the world will be convicted of Sin. It is by the word that is proclaimed by the disciples (followers) of Lord Jesus Christ in this dispensation. Holy Spirit reproves the world of Sin. Make no mistake! Holy Spirit never approaches any unbeliever stealthily.

It is only after sowing the Word of God in the heart of an unbeliever, the Holy Spirit starts His work of convicting the unbeliever of his sin.

"And when he is come, he will reprove the world of sin, and of righteousness, and of judgment" (John 16:8)

"So faith comes from hearing, and hearing through the word of Christ" Romans 10:17 ESV).

It is the hearing of the word of Christ, which goes hand in glove with the Holy Spirit's conviction of Sin, which makes the unbeliever to confess that Jesus is Lord, and believes in his heart that God raised Him from the dead.

The basic Sin of which the world is guilty, is the unbelief in Lord Jesus Christ. Without hearing the Gospel of Jesus Christ, the unbeliever never knows the truth of the word of God, and never does he take into cognizance the sacrifice of Lord Jesus Christ on behalf of him. His mind and understanding is shut towards the truth of the knowledge of true God. It is by first hearing the word of God, and then by the reproving/conviction of the Holy

Spirit that the truth of the knowledge of God is understood by the unbeliever.

In essence it is the joint work of preaching of the Gospel of Jesus Christ, and the conviction of Sin by the Holy Spirit that convinces a sinner that he has transgressed the word of God and, therefore, he needs salvation. Consequently he yields to the Lord and is saved.

CHAPTER 3

WAGES AND RANSOM

"They that trust in their wealth, and boast themselves in the multitude of their riches; none of them can by any means redeem his brother, nor give to God a ransom for him: (For the redemption of their soul is precious, and it ceases forever)" (Psalms 49:6-8)

The word "wages" is a financial term. It is the earnings of someone who did some work for one's employer. The word "ransom" is the amount paid to redeem a prisoner or slave from his/her captivity.

WAGES OF SIN

Bible says...

"For the wages of sin is death; but the gift of God is eternal life through Jesus Christ our Lord". (Romans 6:23)

According to Holy Scriptures "the wages of sin is death"; that is to say a man by committing sin earns death as his wages. Inasmuch as Adam sinned his earning was death. He had his spiritual death instantly and lost fellowship with God. Later, he had his physical death. He was made of dust and to dust he returned.

Physical death is common to believer and unbeliever alike. However, there is significant difference between the death of a believer in Christ, and unbeliever. The believer will rise from the dead with glorified body to be with the Lord Jesus Christ forever and ever and reign with Him. His earnings are eternal life through Lord Jesus Christ and it is a gift of God.

The believer earns his inheritance in heaven by accepting Lord Jesus Christ as his personal savior. Sinner by confession of his sins to Jesus and praying to Him to forgive His sins, and by believing in the resurrection of the Lord earns everlasting life.

The life after death for believer and unbeliever is endures forever, but the former will be happy and spend his everlasting life joyfully not only by being with Lord Jesus Christ, but by reigning with Him forever and ever, while the latter will rise from the dead on the last day, to stand before the "great white throne", where he will be judged by God, who will sentences him to be thrown into the 'lake of fire'.

"Lake of fire" is a place where there will be no end for gnashing of teeth, and where thirst of the punished victim will not be quenched. His inheritance is suffering in the "lake of fire", because God finds him guilty of committing transgression of His commands. The victim never would have prayed to God to forgive his sins and for the redemption of his soul. His portion of earnings is the second death, which is to spend his time in the 'lake of fire'.

REDEMPTION

The children of Israel suffered four hundred years serving as slaves in the land of Egypt under Pharaoh. The LORD heard their cry and promised them deliverance from the bondage of slavery. He said to Moses, to tell the children of Israel that He is the LORD and He will bring them out from under the burdens of the Egyptians. He promised them that He will redeem them with His stretched out arm and will rid them out of their bondage. He will bring great judgment upon Egyptians, He said. (cf. 6:6).

It was physical redemption promised to them. As for spiritual deliverance of mankind from the slavery of sin under the bondage of Satan, God made provision by sending His only begotten Son, Lord Jesus Christ to die as sacrifice on behalf of us, in order that we may accept Jesus as the Savior, and believe in God that He raised Jesus from the dead on the third day.

In the Old Testament period animal sacrifices were made to temporarily cover the sin of the transgressor, but when the fulness of time had come, God sent Jesus into this world in due time to become sacrifice on behalf of us. There is no need for repeated animal sacrifices to be made now. Lord Jesus has willingly become sacrifice on behalf of us once and for all. It pleased the Father to bruise His Son on the cross for our sake. The sins of the Old Testament believers that were covered were expiated by the blood of Jesus Christ, and He became a propitiation for all in the New Testament period. Thus, all those, who believe in Him as personal savior shall be saved.

Scripture says "...the wages of sin is death..." and the redemption of soul of a sinner is possible only by the shedding of the blood of the worthy one, who can deliver sinner from his sin. Sinner is redeemed by accepting Jesus Christ as his/her Lord and savior. Lord Jesus Christ was the only one who was worthy of dying on behalf of us, because He was sent by God into this earth. He is the only mediator, and He is the only high priest.

RANSOM FOR REDEMPTION:

Redemption is of two types; it is of persons and it is of inheritance.

Of persons on this earth, is by paying a sum of money as ransom under the provisions of Exodus 21:1-36; Leviticus 25:25 and 25:48.

"If there be laid on him a sum of money, then he shall give for the ransom of his life whatsoever is laid upon him" (Exodus 21:30)

"If thy brother be waxen poor, and hath sold away some of his possession, and if any of his kin come to redeem it, then shall he redeem that which his brother sold". (Leviticus 25:25)

"After that he is sold he may be redeemed again; one of his brethren may redeem him" (Leviticus 25:48)

However, no one however rich one is, can redeem the soul of one's brother or any close relative unto God by paying ransom. It is possible to redeem one's brother or relative physically from the bondage of slavery or redeem land by paying ransom equivalent to the value set for the man/woman or land; but no human being can redeem the soul of anyone by paying any amount of money or blood. It is possible to redeem the soul of a person by the one, who is worthy to do so; and the only one worthy to take up such task is the incarnate God, Lord Jesus Christ, the Son of God, who came into this world in the form a servant and in the likeness of man.

"None of them can by any means redeem his brother, nor give to God a ransom for him" (Psalms 49:7)

WHO CAN PAY RANSOM?

"For there is one God, and one mediator between God and men, the man Christ Jesus; who gave himself a ransom for all, to be testified in due time" (1 Timothy 2:5-6)

Only kinsman can redeem a slave on this earth. (References: Leviticus 25:28; 25:48)

Blood relative especially male

A relative by marriage

A person of same nationality or ethnicity

A shadow of this kinsman-ship is found in the deliverance of Ruth, who was a Moabites widow, and a daughter-in-law of Naomi. The narration is in the book of Ruth 3:1-13

SPIRITUAL REDEMPTION FROM THE BONDGE OF SIN

Lord Jesus Christ is our kinsman.

"For both he that sanctifies and they who are sanctified are all of one: for which cause he is not ashamed to call them brethren" (Hebrews 2:11)

But when the fulness of the time was come, God sent forth his Son, made of a woman, made under the law, to redeem them that were under the law, that we might receive the adoption of sons. (Galatians 4:4-5)

If Jesus came into this world as an angel He would not have qualified to become sacrifice for our sins, because man is lower than angel, or if He came as some inferior living creature than man, he would not have qualified to become a sacrifice for our sake, because the ransom paid should be of equal to the value of the one who is to be redeemed. The ransom can be either a blood-relative, or a relative by marriage, or of same nationality or ethnicity.

Lord Jesus Christ became little lower than angel and came in the form of a servant and in the likeness of man into this world. He was the "Son of God" and lived a life as "Son of Man" among us.

"But as many as received him, to them gave he power to become the sons of God, even to them that believe on his name" (John 1:12)

"And the Word was made flesh, and dwelt among us, (and we beheld his glory, the glory as of the only begotten of the Father,) full of grace and truth" (John 1:14)

"But when the fulness of the time was come, God sent forth his Son, made of a woman, made under the law, To redeem them that were under the law, that we might receive the adoption of sons" (Galatians 4:4-5)

More details of redemption of property and persons are found in Leviticus 27:9-25; 25:47-55. The book of Ruth details about Kinsman and redemption by kinsman. In Ruth 3:12 and 13 and following verses we see how Boaz redeems Ruth. (Also comparing Exodus 20:2; Psalm 82:4; Daniel 6:27; Jeremiah 20:13, Ezekiel 34:10-12, 22 will show how Jehovah was Israel's Redeemer. He is the Father, and He is the Deliverer and preserver).

In the New Testament we see that Lord Jesus became little lower than angel and came into this world, and identified His people as brethren (cf. Hebrews 2:9, 11). No one can come to Lord Jesus Christ unless the Father, who sent Him draws him. Lord Jesus will raise him up at the last day (cf. John 6:44).

Jesus is the way, the truth and the life. No one comes to the Father except by Him and God desires that all people to be saved and to come to the knowledge of the truth, but only those who confess their sins to Him, and accept Him as Lord and believe in heart that God raised Him from the dead will be saved (John 6:44; John 14:6; 1 Timothy 2:4; 1 John 1:8-10; Romans 10:9-10)

CHAPTER 4

REPROVING BELIEVERS – OF

RIGHTEOUSNESS

HOLY SPIRIT CONVICTS BELIEVERS – OF

RIGHTEOUSNESS

"There is therefore now no condemnation for those who are in Christ Jesus" (Romans 8:1 ESV)

The second action of the Holy Spirit is in, not only leading the sinner to salvation, but His continuing work in believers' hearts assuring them of Christ's righteousness in them. His work primarily is to remind the believer of Christ's imparted (shared) righteousness with them.

Innumerable circumstances arise in the believer's life, where he recollects his past sins and gets disappointed. Satan takes advantage of the weakness of believer, who may repeatedly recollect his past sins. Satan keeps scaring believer by questioning as to how God could save such a great sinner as he is. He would also try to convince believer that his past sins were greater in nature than can be forgiven. It is in these circumstances that Holy Spirit intervenes and assures that there is no condemnation for those who are in Christ Jesus and the Lord's righteousness is imparted on the believer.

The scripture does not say, there is no condemnation for a certain period of time, like few days or months or years, as if penalty in imposed in the court of law for a specified period, and then there is no penalty thereafter; no! The promise from God is that there is no condemnation for indefinite period; that is eternally!

The word "Spirit" indicative of "Holy Spirit" is found 21 times in Romans 8:1-39 signifying the importance of the works of Holy Spirit in believers' lives.

Satan constantly keeps attacking the frail nature of believer, and drags him backwards with disappointments, telling him in his heart that he is not righteous. Satan keeps telling that man can never become righteous. It is hard, he says, and reminds us of our past sins.

It is at this point of time that Holy Spirit very strongly interferes in the life of believer and restores confidence that he is made righteous by the cleansing of his sins in the blood of Jesus Christ. While the Holy Spirit shows to the world, standard of righteousness one has to attain to be saved, His main purpose in the lives of believers is to comfort believers.

By pointing the Lord's righteousness to the unsaved, who hear the word of God, He does not start convicting sinner before word is preached or before the sinner reads the word of God; but He starts convicting him of his failure to abide by the law of God, and his requirement to become righteous in order to be saved and receive everlasting life, only after the word of God is sown in the heart of sinner.

It is after the sinner repents and confesses that Jesus is Lord, and believes in His heart that God raised him from the dead, the Holy Spirit convicts/ reproves/admonishes/assures him that he has attained Christ's righteousness, and there is therefore, he will never be condemned by God.

Bible says we all have sinned and come short of the glory of God. It is by the grace of God through the redemption that is in

Lord Jesus Christ that we are justified freely. God had set forth His only Son to become a sacrifice on behalf of us. It pleased the Father to bruise His only Son for the purpose of redeeming us from the bondage of slavery of sin.

God made provision and promise that whoever believes in Lord Jesus Christ as his/her savior will be forgiven of his sins and will be justified and will be declared as righteous. The repentant sinner will receive remission of his past sins. His past sins will be reckoned as ceased once and for all. The Lord does not remember our past sins anymore after forgiving them. It is Satan, who brings to our memory our past sins to scare us. Once the Lord has forgiven our sins, they are no more remembered.

It is when we are stumbling with this confusion caused by Satan, who causes us to remember our past sins that the Holy Spirit convicts us of Christ's righteousness that we have received. We are declared as having received His unfailing righteousness. (cf. Romans 3:23-26)

Lord Jesus Christ pointed to Himself and set the standard of righteousness a sinner should attain. There is only one, who came down from the Father and lived a life of sinless perfection, and ascended into heaven. He alone can claim that He is perfect. However, when we are born again we receive His righteousness, the standard of which is set by the Lord Himself is shared by the Lord with us. Lord Jesus Christ is the Son of God and He was also called the Son of Man. He was a great intercessor (cf. John 3:13; 1 Timothy 2:5).

In Jesus alone was perfect righteousness. The world said no one can attain that perfectness, but the Lord was righteous and His righteousness is shared with all the believers in the Lord. The righteousness is imparted to us and it was not imputed. The sin was imputed to us when Adam sinned. That is why the Lord has given us assurance that the "law of the Spirit of life" has set us free in Christ Jesus from the "law of sin and death" (cf. Romans 8:2).

Lord Jesus spoke the words that the Father had taught Him. The Lord said He never did anything that was not approved by the Father. Lord Jesus said to His disciples that this realization comes to them when He is lifted up on the cross. Until Jesus was raised from the dead the disciples did not understand much of what the Lord spoke to them.

It is this reason that Lord Jesus Christ said that it is imperative that He goes away to the Father in order that the Holy Spirit comes into their hearts and bring to their remembrance all that the Lord spoke to them. It is this reason that the Holy Spirit is indwelling the believers' hearts and comforting them and admonishing them of Christ's righteousness in them.

In Lord Jesus Christ alone is the fulness of Godhead lives. He alone is the glory of God. It is so pleasant to note that this standard of righteousness of Lord Jesus Christ is imparted to us. (cf. John 8:28; Col. 2:9; Rom. 3:23)

CHAPTER 5

DOES HOLY SPIRIT CONVICT BELIEVERS-

OF SIN

Sometimes we are faced with question if Holy Spirit convicts believers, of sin in order to chastise, or to set us right with God. There is a problem in understanding this aspect. It appears that the Holy Spirit convicts believers in their day-to-day of their inadvertent sinning, or deliberate sinning in some inevitable circumstances. However, that is not true! Holy Spirit never convicts believers, of Sin, He convicts believers, of righteousness.

The moment we read that Holy Spirit convicts, the inference we make of the word "convict" is to hold responsible of an offence, or declare guilty of an offence, especially in a legal case, in the court of law. Bible uses court room scene in the case of "justification" of a believer (a sinner turned righteous).

God justifies a believer that there is no condemnation for him. A sinner, who believes that Jesus is Lord and believes in his heart that God raised him from the dead, is saved eternally and sealed with the promise of Holy Spirit. Seal is an official declaration of a completed transaction.

Holy Spirit is God. He is one among the Triune God. Lord Jesus Christ, who is the second person in the Triune God, ascended into heaven, after He fulfilled all the Scriptures. He died in our stead in order that all those who believe in Him as personal savior, may receive everlasting life, and be with Him forever and ever, when He comes again.

Before the Lord left this earth to be with the Father, He promised that He would pray the Father to send another comforter to be with His followers until the end. Until the end means until the Lord comes again. Holy Spirit descended into this world, as was promised by Lord Jesus Christ, to be in this world, in His stead to help and comfort believers. It is by His seal that our salvation is confirmed and sealed, which is a completed transaction.

CONSCIENCE

It does not need the Holy Spirit to tell you that you have sinned, may it be as trivial as getting angry on someone, or deceiving someone, but know that everyone, irrespective of believer or unbeliever, has conscience, which is a perceive what is right and what is wrong.

Immediately after Adam and Eve sinned they lost fellowship with God. When the LORD visited them in the cool of the day to have fellowship with them, He found them hiding, because they had sense of what is right and what is wrong. They found that they were naked. They were naked before God even before they sinned, but they realized of their nakedness only when they transgressed God's law. They made aprons of fig leaves and hid themselves from God.

The LORD, in His compassion, replaced their aprons made of fig leaves with that of skin of animal, which obviously was sacrificed for them. The bloodshed was essential to condone their sin. The skin of animal was used to wrap their bodies to cover their nakedness. It was God, who made the provision for their reconciliation with Him.

Adam's eldest son, Cain, who did not bring the right offering unto God, killed his younger brother Abel, who's offering was accepted by God. Cain, who killed Abel out of jealousy, incurred God's wrath. The period he lived in was devoid of any written law until the law was given to Moses, and to the people of Israel thereafter. In this period even though they did not have God's written law, they had their conscience to guide them. All those who transgressed their conscience, such as those who lived in Noah's period, and Lot's period, suffered God's wrath by deluge, and fire, respectively.

It is this conscience that brings to remembrance the believer's inadvertent sin, or deliberate sin. The believer is remorseful of his sin and tries to be right with God. It is in this situation that Holy Spirit takes control of believer's desperate condition, and helps him in his prayer.

The Holy Spirit groans in prayer not in unintelligible words, but with intelligible words, according to the Father's will and pleads to forgive him. There is also Lord Jesus Christ, who is seated on the right hand of the Majesty, interceding on behalf of believer, incessantly.

Any repetition of bringing to remembrance the failure of a believer, is Satan's activity. It is Satan, who by reminding sin causes disappointment. The more the believer remembers his past sins, the more he gets dejected; and eventually he ends up in a state of living in depression; but if he pays heed to the voice of the Holy Spirit, he will hear that his sins are forgiven once and for all, and he is freed from the captivity of Satan's vile plans of holding him as slave.

COMFORT

Believers should know that the sin that was upon Jesus, who was crucified on their behalf, was judged at the cross. He was condemned on our behalf already. There is therefore, no condemnation for a believer. Whenever Satan reminds of our sin, we should make it a point to thwart away Satan's activities by calling upon the name of Jesus and His power.

The Holy Spirit helps believer to realize that he is imputed with God's righteousness through Christ. Scripture is clear that a true believer will not keep sinning and sin has no dominion over a believer. If in spite of the existence of scriptures, one sins, then, he is not a true believer. The scripture says if you are angry with someone, reconcile with offended party before the sun goes down. Confess your sins before God and have His forgiveness.

There is nothing that we could do, nor would our good works will earn salvation for us. There are only two ways. One, to be saved and receive salvation free of cost by believing in the efficacy of the blood of Lord Jesus Christ, or chose to live in sin, under the slavery of Satan, who along with his followers will be judged at the great white throne, and cast into the 'lake of fire'.

"In whom ye also trusted, after that ye heard the word of truth, the gospel of your salvation: in whom also after that ye believed, ye were sealed with that Holy Spirit of promise" (Ephesians 1:13)

PERUSAL

It is beyond comprehension that Holy Spirit, who came into this world, to be in the hearts of believers would convict and find them guilty of sin. Holy Spirit convicts the world, of sin, and convicts them, of the judgment. That is what the Scripture says:

"Nevertheless, I tell you the truth: it is to your advantage that I go away, for if I do not go away, the Helper will not come to you. But if I go, I will send him to you. And when he comes, he will convict the world concerning sin and righteousness and judgment: concerning sin, because they do not believe in me; concerning righteousness, because I go to the Father, and you will see me no longer; concerning judgment, because the ruler of this world is judged" (John 16:7-11 ESV)

If we ponder on few relevant verses it becomes clear that while Satan keeps accusing believers every moment not only to disappoint them, but also accusing them before God, as we read in Revelation 12:10; his main purpose is to find little of our time to sneak into, and when we drift slightly away from righteous path, he tempts us; and accuses us immediately rather than wait for a long period of time. Satan keeps saying in our hearts that we no longer deserve God's love.

Satan does not keep waiting until we crawl towards the cliff in sin, and push us down into the valley of destruction then. No, he keeps accusing us all the time. He brings disappointment to us all the time. He keeps accusing us all the time before God.

"And I heard a loud voice in heaven, saying, 'Now the salvation and the power and the kingdom of our God and the authority of his Christ have come, for the accuser of our brothers has been thrown down, who accuses them day and night before our God' " (Revelation 12:10 ESV)

While Satan keeps accusing us brining disappointment in our lives, it is Holy Spirit, who bestows in us confidence, courage and boldness assuring us the presence of God with us, and that we may come before God to pray and seek His help, His forgiveness, and His love. We have already been redeemed by the blood of Lord Jesus Christ, and there is, therefore, no condemnation (cf. Romans 8:1).

HELP FROM HOLY SPIRIT

Holy Spirit will teach us as to what we should do in our weakness and in our falling, and even helps us as to how we should pray. Many times we ask amiss, and do not pray according the will of God. The LORD wants us to pray according to His will. We have no clear picture of our lives, and of our future. God knows everything about us, and He wants us to surrender to His will.

Holy Spirit's works are multifarious in the lives of believers. He intercedes on behalf of us with groaning, not with unintelligible words, but with words that are too deep in nature. He presents our prayers before the Father according to the purposes of God. When we give freedom for Holy Spirit to take charge of our lives and intercede on our behalf, the words that come out of heart and mouth, will emanate from the bottom of our hearts with deep sorrow seeking forgiveness from God. Simultaneously, He brings to our conscience that we have been imputed with God's righteousness in Christ. He infuses confidence in us that no one can condemn us.

Holy Spirit helps victims of persecution with comfort, just as Stephen was given words to speak before high priest.

"But he, being full of the Holy Ghost, looked up steadfastly into heaven, and saw the glory of God, and Jesus standing on the right hand of God" (Acts 7:55)

Believers are encouraged to fear not the ones, who can kill the body but not the soul, but fear the one who has authority to kill not only the body but the soul, as well. God's love is poured into our hearts through the Holy Spirit. He indwells us and comforts believers incessantly. (cf. Eph. 1:7; Romans 5:5; 8:26; Acts 7:55)

CHAPTER 6

REPROVING WORLD – OF JUDGMENT

HOLY SPIRIT CONVICTS WORLD – OF JUDGMENT

If Lord Jesus Christ had not risen from the dead, He would have gone in history just as any other man, who had natural birth and died a natural death. There is no one, except Jesus, on earth born of Virgin and lived a holy life, and died substitutionary death on our behalf. He became propitiation for whole mankind.

Holy Spirit convicts man - of sin, and judgement. The first incidence of such conviction is seen in Acts 2:14-33 when Peter, the disciple of Jesus Christ, preached the Gospel of Jesus Christ.

"Now when they heard this they were cut to the heart, and said to Peter and the rest of the apostles, 'Brothers, what shall we do?'"(Acts 2:37 ESV)

"And Peter said to them, "Repent and be baptized every one of you in the name of Jesus Christ for the forgiveness of your sins, and you will receive the gift of the Holy Spirit (Acts 2:38 ESV)

It is by confession that Jesus is Lord and by believing in heart that God raised Him from the dead only a man can be saved from perishing (cf. Romans 10:9-10).

When Jesus was crucified on the cross it appeared to many people that He was defeated and had no recourse to life. People questioned as to how He, who could not save Himself from the horrendous punishment of crucifixion, can save others from perishing. However, His resurrection from the dead was evidence that death could not hold Him in the grave, and He rose from the dead victoriously. He died according to scriptures and was buried and was raised from the dead according to Scriptures.

By raising Jesus from the dead the Father showed not only to all erstwhile generations but all future generations in the world that Jesus Christ defeated Satan, the Prince of Darkness at the Cross. The devil was judged at the cross and Jesus Christ was victorious.

God has reconciled us to Himself by Jesus Christ. Inasmuch as He did not impute to us our trespasses, but instead committed to us, the word of reconciliation, we proclaim the word of God to others, as well. The power is in the Holy Scriptures. It is not the wisdom or proficiency of man that makes way for the unregenerate to be regenerated; but it is the powerful of the Word of God that brings the change in men.

"For the word of God is living and active, sharper than any two-edged sword, piercing to the division of soul and of spirit, of joints and of marrow, and discerning the thoughts and intentions of the heart" Hebrews 4:12

Apostle Paul said he did not go to Corinth with Excellency of speech with great vocabulary or of wisdom declaring the testimony of God, but with all the weakness, fear and in much trembling. He admonishes us that our faith should not stand emulate the wisdom of men, but in the power of God (cf. 1 Corinthians 2:1-5)

Paul says he was beseeching them like an ambassador for Christ, as though God was beseeching them. He prayed in Christ's stead that they may be reconciled to God, because God had made Jesus Christ, who knew no sin, to be sin for us in order that we might be made the righteousness of God in Him (cf. 2 Corinthians 5:16-21)

"For he hath made him to be sin for us, who knew no sin; that we might be made the righteousness of God in him" (2 Corinthians 5:21)

Therefore, it is evident that our sin that Jesus had to bear upon Himself, was judged at the cross. Lord Jesus was proven innocent at the trial by Pontius Pilate, Governor of Roman Government, and yet Pilate ordered Him to be scourged and delivered to be crucified.

Pilate yielded to the vociferous cry of the Jews, who should repeatedly "Crucify him, crucify him". He was so great a coward that he could not take the decision by himself, but feared the crowd and released Barabbas, a traitor, instead of ordering the release of Jesus. Added to that he, who declared Jesus as innocent, yielded to the cry of the crowd, and delivered Jesus to be crucified.

The death of Jesus on the cross bearing our sin and shame upon Himself, was to reconcile us to the Father. Whoever believes in Him will not be condemned unto death, but will receive glorified bodies and live forever with the Lord Jesus Christ.

As true the Word of God is, surely for those that do not believe in Lord Jesus Christ, there awaits the punishment of suffering in the 'lake of fire'. It is a place, where the gnashing of teeth does not stop, and thirst does not get quenched. This is the judgment for the unsaved men. It is this judgment that the Holy Spirit convicts men of.

"Whoever believes in him is not condemned, but whoever does not believe is condemned already, because he has not believed in the name of the only Son of God" (John 3:18 ESV)

The basis for saying that believers in Christ will not be judged is because Satan, the ruler of this world, is judged at the cross. We who were under the bondage of slavery of sin, and were walking according the whims of Satan, are redeemed by the substitutionary death of Lord Jesus Christ.

Jesus died for our sake paying the penalty of sin. We were debtors to God but Jesus paid our debt and reconciled us to the Father. It is not by silver or gold that we were redeemed but by the blood of Jesus Christ.

God, who is rich in kindness and great in love redeemed us when we were dead in trespasses. The salvation we received is exclusively of God's gift; not of our works. Our sin was judged upon the cross. The believers in Christ will be conformed to His image and will live with Him forever and ever. The Son of God was manifested in order that He might destroy the works of the devil. He defeated the devil at the cross, spoiled principalities and powers. Final destruction of the devil will be when he and his followers are thrown into the 'lake of fire', where gnashing of teeth and thirst cannot be quenched (cf. Colossians 2:15; Mark 9:48; Luke 13:28; 1 John 3:8)

Those, who believe in Jesus are not condemned, but those who do not believe in Him are already condemned; and they will stand before the "great white throne" judgment and will receive punishment for rejecting Jesus as savior (cf. John 16:11; Ephesians 2:2-10)

"And I saw a great white throne, and Him who is sitting upon it, from whose face the earth and the heaven did flee away, and place was not found for them; and I saw the dead, small and great, standing before God, and scrolls were opened, and another scroll was opened, which is that of the life, and the dead were judged out of the things written in the scrolls-- according to their works; and the sea did give up those dead in it, and the death and the hades did give up the dead in them, and they were judged, each one according to their works; and the death and the hades were cast to the lake of the fire--this is the second death; and if anyone was not found written in the scroll of the life, he was cast to the lake of the fire" (Revelation 20:11-15)

The hope for the believers is that Lord Jesus Christ destroyed Satan, and the power of death. He delivered believers in Him to everlasting life. Those, who were subject to lifelong slavery were, upon believing the Lord as their savior, delivered from the suffering in the 'lake of fire' (cf. Hebrews 2:14, 15)

Bible declares that whoever commits sin is of the devil, and whoever confesses Jesus is Lord has the privilege to call the Father as 'Abba, Father' and have the privilege of being called as "sons of God".

"But as many as received him, to them gave he power to become the sons of God, even to them that believe on his name" (John 1:12)

CHAPTER 7

HOLY SPIRIT IN OLD TESTAMENT PERIOD

HOLY SPIRIT'S PRESENCE DURING OLD TESTAMENT PERIOD

As far as general areas such as (1) Regeneration, (2) Restraint, and (3) Empowerment for specific service is concerned, there is no difference of the role of Holy Spirit in believers in the Old Testament period and in the New Testament period. As for the indwelling of Holy Spirit in believers is concerned, there is considerable difference in the Old Testament and in the New Testament.

In the Old Testament period Holy Spirit visited the people of God, irrespective of whether He was to come upon an individual, or upon congregation. Holy Spirit encouraged them and helped them in achieving their purpose. After the purpose for which He came from heaven is achieved, He went back to heaven. Holy Spirit did not continue to stay in this world when He came, but left to be with the Father as soon as the purpose for which He was sent by the Father was fulfilled. There are many examples in the Old Testament but only select few are explained here.

HOLY SPIRIT's ROLE IN REGENERATION

Inasmuch as the Holy Spirit is the living person, we do not refer Him as "it", but we refer Holy Spirit as "Him". He is constantly comforting us, guiding us. He convicts unbelievers by the Gospel message proclaimed by the servants of God, through the reading of the Bible etc. Except for indwelling of the Holy Spirit permanently in the believers of the New Testament His major role in the Old Testament and in the New Testament are similar. Holy Spirit convicts/reproves/admonishes the world of:

- SIN
- RIGHTEOUSNESS
- JUDGMENT

HOLY SPIRIT IS THE RESTRAINER

The Holy Spirit is known as the "Restrainer". His work includes restraining the power of sin, which takes dominance only in the cases where the patience of God towards sinner reaches His maximum tolerant limits.

In Romans 1:21-32 the facts presented are clear evidence as to how man, who glorified himself elevating his knowledge above that of God, is handed over to his sinful nature. Men, who professed themselves that they are wiser than God, have become fools.

They carved images of birds, of four-footed animals, and of reptiles and worshipped them as gods, attributing glory to them instead of recognizing the incorruptible and immutable God. That is the reason why God gave them unto their uncleanness through lusts of their own hearts.

They dishonored their own bodies and altered the truth of God into lies. They worshiped and served creature more than the creator. This is the cause why the Lord gave them over to their own vile affections.

Women changed the natural use into that which is unnatural. Men left the natural use of women and burned their lusts one toward another, and coexisting men resorting to abominable activities, which resulted in reaping compensation for the error that they committed. That is the reason why God gave them up to their vile desires.

Where can man take refuge when God gives upon him? Man finds no solace in either God or Devil. Finally he gets confused and ends up in whoredom, wickedness, covetousness, malice, full of envy, murder, strife, deceit, evil dispositions etc.(cf. Romans 1:20-32)

In the Old Testament period Holy Spirit restrained sin and yet when man crossed the limits of God's tolerance limits he was punished as we read in Genesis 6:3.

God caused it to rain for forty days and forty nights and destroyed the world with flood saving only righteous Noah and his family and also cattle, fowl, and reptiles that God asked him to collect into the ark for them to procreate and replenish.

"And the LORD said, My spirit shall not always strive with man, for that he also is flesh: yet his days shall be an hundred and twenty years" (Genesis 6:3)

"And GOD saw that the wickedness of man was great in the earth, and that every imagination of the thoughts of his heart was only evil continually" (Genesis 6:5)

"And the rain was upon the earth forty days and forty nights" (Genesis 7:12)

Likewise, when man's wickedness reached maximum that God can see, he destroyed Sodom and Gomorrah.

"Then the LORD rained on Sodom and Gomorrah sulfur and fire from the LORD out of heaven. (Genesis 19:24)

The Bible speaks of Holy Spirit restraining sin in 2 Thessalonians 2:3-8

"Let no one deceive you in any way. For that day will not come, unless the rebellion comes first, and the man of lawlessness is revealed, the son of destruction, who opposes and exalts himself against every so-called god or object of worship, so that he takes his seat in the temple of God, proclaiming himself to be God. Do you not remember that when I was still with you I told you these things? And you know what is restraining him now so that he may be revealed in his time. For the mystery of lawlessness is already at work. Only he who now restrains it will do so until he is out of the way. And then the lawless one will be revealed, whom the Lord Jesus will kill with the breath of his mouth and bring to nothing by the appearance of his coming" 2 Thessalonians 2:3-8

We are able to sustain the power of sin because Holy Spirit is restraining Satan from enforcing his temptations on us. Unless, God's immaculate and powerful protection is removed from us Satan cannot be triumphant on a child of God. However, there will come a time Holy Spirit, the restrainer, will be removed from this sinful world and it is that time that Satan goes enforcing all his desires and satanic activities in men.

It is therefore, imperative that we obey God and seek His refuge in order that we will be "caught up" when the Lord comes again. The Lord will not allow His flock to suffer any damage from the fierce attacks of Satan.

On the contrary, in the New Testament period Holy Spirit is the Promise given by the Father to the believer to be with him and in him forever until the believer breathes his last.

"In him you also, when you heard the word of truth, the gospel of your salvation, and believed in him, were sealed with the promised Holy Spirit" (Ephesians 1:13)

EMPOWERMENT FOR SPECIFIC SERVICE

One of the three general functions of the Holy Spirit is also the ability He grants to the servants of God to service to the Godhead. Although not similar to those of the New Testament Spiritual gifts, as we see in 1 Corinthians 12:4-11, yet the endowment of Spiritual gifts by the Holy Spirit were evident in the Old Testament as well; such as the gift of artwork given to Bezalel by the Holy Spirit as recorded in Exodus 31:2-5. Bezalel was an exceptional workman in the construction of the Tabernacle. Exceptional capabilities to govern the nation of Israel, were given to Saul, David, and Solomon by the Holy Spirit. The unique function of the Holy Spirit, which is exclusive to the New Testament believers is His permanent indwelling in the hearts of New Testament believers.

"And I have filled him with the spirit of God, in wisdom, and in understanding, and in knowledge, and in all manner of workmanship" (Exodus 31:3)

The Holy Spirit also was responsible in the New Creation as we read in 2 Corinthians 5:17. Holy Spirit is constantly convicting unbelievers of their sin, righteousness and judgement through the service of the God's servants in their regeneration. More and more people are coming into the kingdom of God. Old things in regenerated man will pass away and all things in him become new instantly as he accepts Jesus as Lord and believes in heart that God raised Him from the dead. (Romans 10:9-10)

"Therefore, if anyone is in Christ, he is a new creation. The old has passed away; behold, the new has come" -2 Corinthians 5:17

However, as far as the Holy Spirit's indwelling is concerned, during the Old Testament period, and in the New Testament period, the major differences are very clear. Whereas the New Testament teaches that the Holy Spirit's indwelling in believers is permanent, the Old Testament teaches that the Holy Spirit came upon certain individuals like Joshua, David etc. and departed after the purpose for which He descended is fulfilled, or when the individual lost favor with the LORD God. Nevertheless, the Holy Spirit's coming upon certain people of God does not vouch for the spiritual condition of them, such as Holy Spirit coming upon King Saul, Samson, and many of the Judges.

HOLY SPIRIT IN JOSHUA

"So the LORD said to Moses, 'Take Joshua the son of Nun, a man in whom is the Spirit, and lay your hand on him'" Numbers 27:18

HOLY SPIRIT IN SAUL

In the following two verses we see Holy Spirit's indwelling in Saul but departing from him later on.

"When they came to Gibeah, behold, a group of prophets met him, and the Spirit of God rushed upon him, and he prophesied among them" 1 Samuel 10:10

"Now the Spirit of the LORD departed from Saul, and a harmful spirit from the LORD tormented him" 1 Samuel 16:14

HOLY SPIRIT IN SAMSON

Judges 14:1-16; 15:14; 16:28 have the details about Samson's rise and fall consequent upon Holy Spirit's dwelling in him and departing from him.

HOLY SPIRIT AMONG ISRAELITES

"And they came, everyone whose heart stirred him, and everyone whose spirit moved him, and brought the LORD's contribution to be used for the tent of meeting, and for all its service, and for the holy garments" Exodus 35:21

When the need arose to build Tabernacle, have material for it, and garments for the priests, the children of Israel were moved in their hearts by the Holy Spirit to contribute to buy those materials. They all brought their contributions to the LORD at the tent of meeting, and for its service, and the holy garments.

HOLY SPIRIT IN DAVID

"And he sent and brought him in. Now he was ruddy and had beautiful eyes and was handsome. And the LORD said, "Arise, anoint him, for this is he." Then Samuel took the horn of oil and anointed him in the midst of his brothers. And the Spirit of the LORD rushed upon David from that day forward. And Samuel rose up and went to Ramah" 1 Samuel 16:12, 13

"Cast me not away from your presence, and take not your Holy Spirit from me" Psalm 51:11

David repented of his sin when Nathan the prophet pointed to him about his adultery with Bathsheba. He prayed very earnestly to God to forgive him of his sin. David said in his prayer that he has sinned against God and his sin was every before him. He prayed to God to purge him with hyssop, and had faith that God will forgive his sin, and he will be whiter that the snow. He prayed to God not to cast away him from the LORD's presence and not to take away Holy Spirit from him.

His prayer indicates that he knew that Holy Spirit would not stay with him or with anyone forever in the lives of the people of God. He knew that Holy Spirit visited God's people and went back to heavenly abode after helping them or after intended purpose of His visit was achieved (cf. Psalm 51:7-11)

HOLY SPIRIT IN CONTRITE HEARTS

"For thus says the One who is high and lifted up, who inhabits eternity, whose name is Holy: "I dwell in the high and Holy place, and also with him who is of a contrite and lowly spirit, to revive the spirit of the lowly, and to revive the heart of the contrite" Isaiah 57:15

Jehovah, who inhabits eternity, and whose name is "Holy", says that the Spirit of God lives in Holy place and also with one who is of a contrite and lowly spirit, to revive the spirit of the lowly and to revive the heart of the contrite.

ISAIAH PLEADS ON BEHALF OF ISRAELITES

"But they rebelled and grieved his Holy Spirit; therefore he turned to be their enemy, and himself fought against them" Isaiah 63:10

The children of Israel repeatedly angered God by disobeying His commandments and Statutes, and therefore, God like their enemy destroyed their peace and swallowed up their palaces, destroyed their strong holds and increased their mourning and lamentation (cf. Isa.63:10; Ps 78:40; 95:10; Ac 7:51; Eph. 4:30; Heb. 3:10,17; Lam. 2:5)

HOLY SPIRIT IN ISAIAH

"Then he remembered the days of old, of Moses and his people. Where is he who brought them up out of the sea with the shepherds of his flock? Where is he who put in the midst of them his Holy Spirit" Isaiah 63:11

Isaiah mentions of the love of God and the fellowship of Holy Spirit that was there with them. He feels bad because the Holy Spirit, who gave courage to Moses to split the Red Sea into two, and helped the people of Israel to boldly walk on the dry ground in the midst of the parted Red Sea, had left them and gone to be with the Father.

Notwithstanding, Isaiah believes that the compassion of the LORD overtakes His anger that the LORD has shown against the children of Israel for their disobedience. He knows that the LORD still remembers the unconditional covenant He made with Abraham. The LORD has undying love for them and remembers the days when Moses the LORD's servant led them through the Red Sea, and wilderness, and shepherded them pleading on their behalf to the LORD.

The prophet, therefore, pleads with God for His mercy toward them. The LORD, who delivered them from the bondage of slavery from Egypt and led Moses, and the children of Israel through the Red Sea is no more with them as their help (cf. Isa. 63:11).

HOLY SPIRIT IN DANIEL

"At last Daniel came in before me—he who was named Belteshazzar after the name of my god, and in whom is the spirit of the holy gods—and I told him the dream, saying" Daniel 4:8

"O Belteshazzar, chief of the magicians, because I know that the spirit of the holy gods is in you and that no mystery is too difficult for you, tell me the visions of my dream that I saw and their interpretation" Daniel 4:9

In his testimony, Nebuchadnezzar mentions of Holy Spirit in Daniel, who was also known as "Belteshazzar". He says that he knew the Spirit of God was in him, and that no mystery was too difficult for him. He also says that all the wise men in his kingdom could not make known to him the interpretation of the dream he dreamt. Thereafter, the king tells Daniel his dream and asks for interpretation of it.

Daniel by the power of Holy Spirit interprets the king's dream as revealed to him by God. The interpretation of the dream was scary and offensive to the king, but Daniel was not reluctant to tell him the truth. He said that it is a decree from the Most High God and it has come upon him that he will be driven among men, and his living will be with the beasts of the field. He said the king shall be made to eat grass like an ox, and he shall be wet with the dew of heaven.

Seven periods of time shall pass over him until he knows that the Most High rules the kingdom of men and gives it to the one whom will desires to give. Daniel says leaving the stump of the roots of the tree confirms that his kingdom will be restored to him as soon as he realizes that the God of heaven, the Most High rules, and not Nebuchadnezzar.

After interpreting the dream, Daniel also becomes very bold by the power of the Holy Spirit, and warns the king to repent and practice righteousness, and discard his iniquities and to show mercy to the oppressed in order that his life may be lengthened and be prosperous.

Just as Daniel interpreted the dream, every event came live in the life of Nebuchadnezzar and when he repented of his sin he was restored to his normal senses and his kingdom was restored to him. (Daniel 4:8-37)

HOLY SPIRIT'S HELP DURING BELSHAZZAR'S DAYS

"There is a man in your kingdom in whom is the spirit of the holy gods. In the days of your father, light and understanding and wisdom like the wisdom of the gods were found in him, and King Nebuchadnezzar, your father—your father the king—made him chief of the magicians, enchanters, Chaldeans, and astrologers" Daniel 5:11

During the days of King Belshazzar's days, he once made a great feast, wherein he took pride in drinking wine in gold and silver vessels that his father Nebuchadnezzar brought from the temple that was in Jerusalem, and praised the gods of gold, and of silver, of brass, of iron, of wood, and of stone. In that hour came forth fingers of the hand of a man and wrote on the wall of king's palace. The king saw what was being written, and his countenance changed immediately and his thoughts troubled him. The joints of his loins loosened, and his knees smote one against another.

The King called enchanters, Chaldeans, soothsayers and wise men from Babylon, and said if any man could interpret the writing on the wall he will put on him purple robe, bracelet of gold on his neck, and will give him the third of his kingdom to rule. None of the king's wise men could read the writing nor could interpret that which was written on the wall. The king was saddened beyond any measure. However, the queen consoled him and said to him that there was a man in his kingdom, who had the Spirit of God, and interpreted the dreams of his father, and asserted that all those interpretations came true.

The king was pleased with the queen's encouragement and called Daniel and said to him that he heard Daniel had the Holy Spirit in him, and, therefore, would give all the gifts he promised if he revealed the mystery of the writing on the wall. However, Daniel answered the king and said to him that he may keep back for himself, or give them to someone else all those gifts he promised to give. Nevertheless, he said he would interpret the writing on the wall for the glory of the living and Most High God.

He narrated as to how his father Nebuchadnezzar, who was given a great kingdom by God, took pride in himself, rather than give glory to the LORD, and therefore, the LORD brought him down from his eminence and drove him from the sons of men. God made the king to live among wild beasts, and eat herb like oxen did till he realized that the Most high God, Jehovah rules the kingdom of men, and the LORD raises whom he will.

Pointing to King Belshazzar, Daniel warned him that he was like his father in all his deeds, and did not humble his heart before the Most High God, Jehovah. He said to the King that because lifted up himself to the level of God instead of honoring in his breath, and in all ways the living and mighty God, Jehovah, his days are numbered by the LORD. The writing was "... MENE, MENE, TEKEL, and PARSIN" which meant God has numbered the days of king's kingdom and brought to an end. He has been weighed in the balances and found wanting, Therefore, his kingdom is divided and given to the Medes and Persians".

Even though Daniel refused to have any gifts from the Belshazzar, he clothed Daniel with scarlet and put a chain of gold around his neck and made proclamation that he should be the third ruler in the kingdom.

Daniel's interpretation came true and in the same night Belshazzar the Chaldean king was killed and Darius the Mede received the kingdom when he was sixty two years old (cf. Daniel 5:26-31)

Thus God used Daniel, by the His Spirit, to enlighten the proud kings, and the people of his kingdom of the futility of man's pride and the consequences of dishonoring the living God.

CHAPTER 8

HOLY SPIRIT IN THE NEW TESTAMENT

First of all, Holy Spirit is not inanimate object to refer to Him as "it" but He is a living person in us, the Spirit of God, and therefore, He is always referred to as 'Him'. In order to understand better who Holy Spirit is it is much helpful if we know the different names He is identified as. There are number of titles given to Him, and few of them are listed below:

- The Spirit of God (Matt. 10:20)
- Another Comforter (John 14:16)
- The Spirit of the Truth (John 14:17)
- The Spirit of Christ (Romans 8:9)
- The Spirit of Adoption (Romans 8:15)
- The Spirit of the Living God (2 Cor. 3:3)
- The Holy Spirit of Promise (Eph.1:13)
- The Spirit of Jesus Christ (Phil. 1:19)
- The Eternal Spirit (Heb.9:14)
- The Spirit of Grace (Heb.10:29)

The prophecies about Lord Jesus incarnation are mentioned in the Law Books of Pentateuch, Prophets, and Historical books of the Bible. Apart from Josephus, a Jewish Historian had also mentioned about Lord Jesus Christ in his writings.

"Now there was about this time Jesus, a wise man, if it be lawful to call him a man; for he was a doer of wonderful works, a teacher of such men as receive the truth with pleasure. He drew over to him both many of the Jews and many of the Gentiles. He was [the] Christ. And when Pilate, at the suggestion of the principal men amongst us, had condemned him to the cross, (9) those that loved him at the first did not forsake him; for he appeared to them alive again the third day; (10) as the divine prophets had foretold these and ten thousand other wonderful things concerning him. And the tribe of Christians, so named from him, are not extinct at this day" "Antiquities of the Jews - Book XVIII: Chapter 3 Paragraph 3

Gospel writer Matthew writes...

"This was to fulfill what was spoken by the prophet Isaiah: Behold, my servant whom I have chosen, my beloved with whom my soul is well pleased. I will put my Spirit upon him, and he will proclaim justice to the Gentiles. He will not quarrel or cry aloud, nor will anyone hear his voice in the streets; a bruised reed he will not break, and a smoldering wick he will not quench, until he brings justice to victory; and in his name the Gentiles will hope." Matthew 12:17-21

This prophecy is in Old Testament Book Isaiah 41:1-9

"1 Behold my servant, whom I uphold, my chosen, in whom my soul delights; I have put my Spirit upon him; he will bring forth justice to the nations. 2 He will not cry aloud or lift up his voice, or make it heard in the street; 3 a bruised reed he will not break, and a faintly burning wick he will not quench; he will faithfully bring forth justice. 4 He will not grow faint or be discouraged till he has established justice in the earth; and the coastlands wait for his law. 5 Thus says God, the Lord, who created the heavens and stretched them out, who spread out the earth and what comes from it, who gives breath to the people on it and spirit to those who walk in it: 6 "I am the Lord; I have called you in righteousness; I will take you by the hand and keep you; I will give you as a covenant for the people, a light for the nations,

7 to open the eyes that are blind, to bring out the prisoners from the dungeon, from the prison those who sit in darkness. 8 I

am the Lord; that is my name; my glory I give to no other, nor my praise to carved idols. 9 Behold, the former things have come to pass, and new things I now declare; before they spring forth I tell you of them."

THE SPIRIT OF GOD

"For it is not you who speak, but the Spirit of your Father speaking through you" Matthew 10:20

Lord Jesus Christ speaks to His disciples and says to them that their road ahead in the ministry of Gospel is not easy path, but would be filled with hardship, trials and troubles. In one of the subsequent verses the Lord says that whoever does not take his cross and follow the Lord is not worthy of Him (cf. Matthew 10:38).

The Lord prepares His disciples for a long time touch ministry not only among the children of Israel, but also among the Gentiles. In preparing them for the ministry He warns them that they are being sent as sheep in the midst of wolves. One can only imagine how tough for the sheep to survive among the wolves that could devour them any time. The sheep are humble creatures that follow their leader and wolves are known to be voracious. The Lord says to them in doing ministry among the voracious wolves they should be as wise as serpents but innocent as doves. The paradigm involves in understanding how cunning the serpent was in the Garden of Eden to achieve his purpose while talking to Eve, and yet the Lord says His disciples should be as innocent as doves; not practicing cheating in their ministry among the oppressors and persecutors (cf. Genesis 3:1; Ps. 58:4–5; Hosea 7:11)

Lord Jesus Christ is the good shepherd of His followers, and He goes before them. The sheep follow Him because they know His voice. The good shepherd lays down His life for the sheep (cf. John 10:3, 4 &11).

While the disciples are on their ministry of Gospel the persecutors would deliver them over to courts and flog them. They would drag them before the secular authorities inasmuch as they bear witness before them and the Gentiles. The Lord assures His protection and consoles them that they need not be anxious as to what they should speak when they are before the authorities. They will be given the words that they should speak at the very moment when they were to defend themselves and speak for the Lord.

The Lord says that when they speak before persecutors and authorities, the Spirit of the Father will speak through them for them.

Brother may deliver brother over to death, the father may deliver his child, and children may rise against parents and commend them to the death, but the one who endures until the end will be saved, says the Lord. This has connotation to Matthew 24:9, 2 Timothy. 2:11–13 and Jude 21

In the context of ministry of the Gospel of Jesus Christ to proclaim to the world the good news that Lord Jesus Christ is the savior of the world, and salvation is in Him and none else, it is seen that The Holy Spirit is the Spirit of God, who speaks for us when we are in trouble.

CHAPTER 9

ANOTHER COMFORTER

"And I will pray the Father, and he shall give you another Comforter, that he may abide with you forever; Even the Spirit of truth; whom the world cannot receive, because it sees him not, neither knoweth him: but ye know him; for he dwelleth with you, and shall be in you. (John 14:16, 17 KJV)

"And I will ask the Father, and he will give you another Helper, to be with you forever, even the Spirit of truth, whom the world cannot receive, because it neither sees him nor knows him. You know him, for he dwells with you and will be in you. (John 14:16, 17 ESV)

The moment we hear that there is another comforter it occurs to our mind that there was already a comforter, who is referring to another comforter.

KJV translation of Greek Strong's Number 3875. "Parakleto" is Comforter, while ESV translated "Parakleto" as the Helper. Fundamentally the meaning and the purpose of "Parakleto" is to intercede or advocate, or to be as comforter. Holy Spirit Is called not only as "Comforter" but also as "Spirit of truth".

Lord Jesus Christ, who was an interceder and an advocate for us, is the only mediator between men and God. He is our High priest and there is no mediator or High priest for us to plead on behalf of us with the Father.

John 17:1-26 (entire chapter) is a great intercessory prayer of Lord Jesus Christ. Hebrews chapters 2-13 show how the Lord has fulfilled the conditions of High Priest and become our High Priest. Galatians 3:19,20; 1 Timothy 2:5; Hebrews 8:6; 9:15;

12:24 say that Jesus is the mediator of the New Covenant. He is our High Priest, and the only Mediator.

Jesus Christ died on behalf of all of us and was buried, and yet the death had no power over Him. He conquered death and rose from the dead on the third day and after staying on this earth for forty days, has ascended into heaven and is seated on the right of the Father. Now, He is constantly pleading on behalf of us in order that we are made perfect and righteous before we step into our eternal abode.

Before Lord Jesus Christ ascended into heaven He comforted His disciples that after He has gone to the Father He will ask Him to send another comforter to be with His disciples, as also with us forever. His followers will not be left out like orphans, but He will be with them forever, He said.

Lord Jesus Christ, who was in the form of God, thought it not robbery to be equal with God but made Himself of no reputation, and took upon Him the form of a servant and was made in the likeness of man (cf. Phil. 2:5-11). He had a physical body and Spirit of God lived in Him. He was the "Son of God", and was also called "Son of Man". The Scriptures say no one has ever seen God but the Son of God has revealed the Father. After He had gone to the Father, Holy Spirit, who has no physical body, was sent into this world by the Father.

Insofar as the function of Lord Jesus Christ, and the Holy Spirit with reference to intercession is similar Holy Spirit is another comforter of the same kind and not of different kind. While Lord Jesus Christ is interceding on behalf of us in heaven, Holy Spirit is comforting and interceding on behalf of us from within our hearts.

When Lord Jesus Christ said to His disciples that the "Comforter" would take His place on this earth to comfort, console, and help His people, and convict unbelievers of Sin,

Righteousness, and Justice, He was referring to John 14:26, where He identifies Comforter as the Holy Spirit.

"But the Helper, the Holy Spirit, whom the Father will send in my name, he will teach you all things and bring to your remembrance all that I have said to you" (John 14:26 ESV)

Jesus Christ also said that Holy Spirit, whom the Lord will send to them from the Father, the Holy Spirit will proceed from the Father and He will bear witness about Him. John 15:26 also says that He is the "Spirit of the truth". Holy Spirit is the Spirit and not visible. Holy Spirit is the Spirit of Lord Jesus Christ Himself.

The Lord said that it is to their advantage that He goes away to the Father, because if He does not return to the Father, from whom He came into this world, His Spirit will not come to them, but if He goes, He will send the Holy Spirit to them. The role of Lord Jesus Christ then would be to plead to the Father on our behalf being seated on the right hand of the Majesty. The role of the Holy Spirit to indwell believers' heart and help them glorify Lord Jesus Christ, and the Father, and to teach His disciples the mysteries of the Kingdom of God.

"But when the Helper comes, whom I will send to you from the Father, the Spirit of truth, who proceeds from the Father, he will bear witness about me" (John 15:26 ESV)

"Nevertheless, I tell you the truth: it is to your advantage that I go away, for if I do not go away, the Helper will not come to you. But if I go, I will send him to you" (John 16:7 ESV)

CHAPTER 10

SHOULD WE WAIT FOR HOLY SPIRIT?

"And I will pray the Father, and he shall give you another Comforter, that he may abide with you forever; Even the Spirit of truth; whom the world cannot receive, because it sees him not, neither knoweth him: but ye know him; for he dwelleth with you, and shall be in you" (John 14:16-17) "I will not leave you comfortless: I will come to you". (John 14:18)

"But the Comforter, which is the Holy Ghost, whom the Father will send in my name, he shall teach you all things, and bring all things to your remembrance, whatsoever I have said unto you. Peace I leave with you, my peace I give unto you: not as the world giveth, give I unto you. Let not your heart be troubled, neither let it be afraid" (John 14:26-27)

The last portion of John 14:17 says "He dwelleth with you, and shall be in you". That is, Holy Spirit was with us when we are born-again, and He is in us from the time when we are born-again. Notice the words of Lord Jesus. He said...

"Jesus saith unto him, I am the way, the truth, and the life: no man cometh unto the Father, but by me". (John 14:6) "... no one cometh unto the Father, but by me".

The Lord will not leave us comfortless.

The Comforter, who is the Holy Spirit, whom the Father sent in Jesus' name, is teaching us and will teach us all things.

WHY THEN PAUL ASKED FEW MEN IN EPHESUS IF THEY HAVE RECEIVED HOLY SPIRIT WHEN THEY BELIEVED?

"And it came to pass, that, while Apollos was at Corinth, Paul having passed through the upper coasts came to Ephesus: and finding certain disciples, He said unto them, have ye received the Holy Ghost since ye believed? And they said unto him, we have not so much as heard whether there be any Holy Ghost. And he said unto them, unto what then were ye baptized? And they said, Unto John's baptism. Then said Paul, John verily baptized with the baptism of repentance, saying unto the people, that they should believe on him which should come after him, that is, on Christ Jesus. When they heard this, they were baptized in the name of the Lord Jesus. And when Paul had laid his hands upon them, the Holy Ghost came on them; and they spoke with tongues, and prophesied. And all the men were about twelve". (Acts 19:1-7) [Emphasis mine]

HAVE YOU RECEIVED HOLY SPIRIT SINCE YOU BELIEVED?

WHAT WAS PAUL ASKING AND WHAT ANSER THEY GAVE?

From their answer it is very much evident that they were not believers in Jesus Christ. If they were believers in Christ, they would have been led by Holy Spirit and in them would Holy Spirit lived, and they would have known about that fact. They said they were baptized unto John's baptism. But John Himself said the one (Jesus) who comes after him is greater than Himself. John's baptism was not of faith in Jesus Christ but of repentance. Obviously they were not of Jesus Christ, but of John.

Romans 8:9, and 1 Corinthians 6:19 show that if a person does not have the Holy Spirit, then he does not belong to Christ.

It is when they said that they were baptized unto John, Paul said to them that they should believe on Jesus Christ. When they heard this fact, they were baptized in the name of Lord Jesus. When Paul laid hands on them, Holy Spirit came on them, and they spoke tongues, which are languages understood by everyone as we read in Acts 2:9-11. They all gathered on the occasion of Passover festival on the day of Pentecost, which is 50th day after resurrection of Lord Jesus Christ.

Parthians, and Medes, and Elamites, and the dwellers in Mesopotamia, and in Judaea, and Cappadocia, in Pontus, and Asia, Phrygia, and Pamphylia, in Egypt, and in the parts of Libya about Cyrene, and strangers of Rome, Jews and proselytes, Cretes and Arabians, who spoke different languages, understood the languages of one another. (Ref. Acts 2:9-11)

"And even things without life giving sound, whether pipe or harp, except they give a distinction in the sounds, how shall it be known what is piped or harped? For if the trumpet give an uncertain sound, who shall prepare himself to the battle? So likewise ye, except ye utter by the tongue words easy to be understood, how shall it be known what is spoken? for ye shall speak into the air" (1 Corinthians 14:7-9)

CHAPTER 11

LAVISHLY ABUNDANT WATER

"And I saw a new heaven and a new earth: for the first heaven and the first earth were passed away; and there was no more sea" (Revelation 21:1)

The exuberant presence of water in eternity is supported by John 4:14; Revelation 21:6; Revelation 22:1; Revelation 22:17, and thus the thought that there will no water based on the phrase that "there was no more sea" in Revelation 21:1, is thwarted away.

It is true as the Word of God says that there will not be sea but there will be plenty of water and in fact, plenty of water of life.

"And he shewed me a pure river of water of life, clear as crystal, proceeding out of the throne of God and of the Lamb" (Revelation 22:1)

The absence of sea in New Jerusalem, and the presence of river therein are blessing to the saved. Going by the phrase "there was no more sea", many would think that there will be no water in eternity; but it is not so.

Old Testament uses the pictures of river as also of water many-a-time to depict the blessings of the Lord. However, the rivers about which the scriptures mentions, are neither allegorical nor symbolical but are real.

The angel showed to John the river of water of life, which was bright as crystal and it flowed from the throne of God, and of Lord Jesus Christ through the middle of the street of the holy city New Jerusalem.

There went out of Garden of Eden to water the garden a river which parted into four heads; the first one was Psion, Second River was Gihon, the third river was Hiddekel, and the fourth was river Euphrates. There went up mist from the earth and watered the whole face of the ground; obviously it did not rain in the beginning, and the plants were watered by the mist that went up the earth. Man and woman lived in this wonderful Garden of Eden.

Each river encompassed certain portion of land. Unique among was Pison, which encompassed the whole land of Havilah, where gold of good quality was found. It also had precious stones viz. bdellium and the onyx stone.

Man's disobedience and transgression of God's commandment caused the ground to be cursed by God, and the Garden of Eden was once for fall shut for them.

When Adam and Eve sinned, there arose the necessity of their redemption from their transgression in order that they may be reconciled to God. The future redemption of mankind by the blood of Lord Jesus Christ, whose sacrifice was alone the perfect sacrifice, is seen in the shadow of covering of their sin by the first act of God, when He removed their self-made aprons made of fig leaves, and replacing them by the skin of animal that was killed and by the blood that was shed (cf. Genesis 3:7; 3:21).

"Unto Adam also and to his wife did the LORD God make coats of skins, and clothed them" (Genesis 3:21)

That is the reason why God sent His one and only Son Jesus Christ into this world in order to take upon Himself our sin and die in our stead. Lord Jesus died on behalf of us on the cross of Calvary and was buried and raised on the third day.

"For God so loved the world, that he gave his only begotten Son, that whosoever believeth in him should not perish, but have everlasting life" (John 3:16)

"For when we were yet without strength, in due time Christ died for the ungodly" (Romans 5:6)

God gave us, who received and believed Lord Jesus Christ as our personal savior, the power to become the sons of God.

"But as many as received him, to them gave he power to become the sons of God, even to them that believe on his name" (John 1:12)

Lord Jesus's body did not remain in the grave nor did see corruption in the grave. Before His death, the Lord said...

"Therefore doth my Father love me, because I lay down my life, that I might take it again? No man taketh it from me, but I lay it down of myself. I have power to lay it down, and I have power to take it again. This commandment have I received of my Father" (John 10:17-18)

God raised Him from the dead on the third day of His crucifixion.

"He is not here: for he is risen, as he said. Come, see the place where the Lord lay" (Matthew 28:6)

After forty days of His resurrection from the dead, Lord Jesus Christ ascended into heaven. He will come back in the same manner as He ascended into heaven.

God forgives sins of all those who confess their sins to Him in the name of Lord Jesus Christ and ask forgiveness. Bible says confess by mouth that Jesus is Lord and believe in heart that God raised Him from the dead on the third day and you will be saved (cf. Romans 10:9-10). The Lord says...

"And, behold, I come quickly; and my reward is with me, to give every man according as his work shall be" (Revelation 22:12)

CHAPTER 12

RECONCILIATION

And without controversy great is the mystery of godliness: God was manifest in the flesh, justified in the Spirit, seen of angels, preached unto the Gentiles, believed on in the world, received up into glory. (1 Timothy 3:16)

But we speak the wisdom of God in a mystery, even the hidden wisdom, which God ordained before the world unto our glory: (1 Corinthians 2:7)

Man was created in the image of God, and yet he lost his fellowship with God because he sinned against the Almighty God by transgressing His command. Yet, God's love for mankind is incredible, unfathomable, in that He offered His own Son to die as substitutionary death on behalf of sinners.

The first covering of the sin of the first man, Adam, was by providing Him clothes made of the skin of an animal that was killed by God, and its blood was shed in order to reconcile man to God. Man's nakedness was covered by the skin clothes by God, who removed their self-made aprons of fig leaves.

God saw that the covering they made for their sin was not enough, but there was a necessity of blood to be shed as substitution. This was the type of substitution that God showed as necessary to cover sins. Later in the books of Exodus and Leviticus details are shown as to how 'Sin offering' and 'Trespass offering' are to be made to cover sins of the transgressors.

Man is imputed with the original sin committed by Adam and, therefore, everyone on this earth, being the offspring of Adam, is imputed with sin. Bible says...

"For all have sinned, and come short of the glory of God" (Romans 3:23)

"If we say that we have no sin, we deceive ourselves, and the truth is not in us. If we confess our sins, he is faithful and just to forgive us our sins, and to cleanse us from all unrighteousness. If we say that we have not sinned, we make him a liar, and his word is not in us" (1 John 1:8-10)

It is this reason why God sent His one and only Son into this world that anyone who believes that Jesus is Lord, and confesses his sins to the Lord, and believes in heart that God raised Him from the dead will be saved and receive everlasting life.

Lord Jesus Christ, in whom we trust and depend for all the good in our lives, is our Savior. God knows our frame and how feeble frail and fallible we are. He knows that we are made of dust and return to dust, and, therefore, he is compassionate and loving always.

The Lord gives us many opportunities, and great deal of time to repent of our sins, and come to Him, and yet if we resist His calling, we are left to our own ways and destiny; and that destination is not a pleasant one.

It is a place called "lake of fire", where neither gnashing of one's teeth ceases, nor will one's thirst quench. There is no end of life there even though one does aspire for it so ardently. But for those who believe in Him, the Lord gives everlasting joyous life to be with Him in glorified bodies forever and ever.

Man's troubles and trials and God's guidance and His providence for one's life. Evaluation of his life from the time he was born to the time when he became a ruler in Egypt

It gives us great insight when we read Joseph's life story and evaluate his life from the time when he was born to the times when he became ruler in Egypt. Though many call it a 'story', yet it is not a fiction or a 'story' told to children but this is a reality that happened in the ancient days, when God chose Abraham, Isaac, and Jacob as his own people. God blessed Abraham and his posterity.

"But ye are a chosen generation, a royal priesthood, an holy nation, a peculiar people; that ye should shew forth the praises of him who hath called you out of darkness into his marvelous light:" 1Peter 2:9 Speaking about Himself, the prophecy in Psalms 22:9, which reads as,

"But thou art he that took me out of the womb: thou didst make me hope when I was upon my mother's breasts" shows us the confidence our Savior Lord Jesus Christ, in the Father in heaven. Great confidence is shown by Psalmist who wrote in Psalms 71:6 that

"By thee have I been holden up from the womb: thou art he that took me out of my mother's bowels: my praise shall be continually of thee".

For those who believe in Jesus everything works for good. "And we know that all things work together for good to them that love God, to them who are the called according to his purpose". Romans 8:28

This is true in the life of Joseph and the same is true in our lives as well.

To Abraham were born, Ishmael, through his hand maid, Hagar, and Isaac, through his wife, Sarah, in their very old age, as a blessing from God. Isaac had two children; Esau, and Jacob. Esau was not chosen by God, but Jacob was chosen one. Each time we read Joseph's story, which is a reality, and his life it generates new and fresh thoughts in us. It is as fresh as ever.

Joseph was born to Rachel, when she was in humiliation for having no children, and Leah; Joseph's first wife had children. Joseph walked on rough road all through his life.

After Dinah was born to Leah through Jacob, Rachel, the second wife of Jacob was feeling very depressed, and prayed to God. "And God remembered Rachel, and God hearkened to her, and opened her womb". Genesis 30:22 When a son was born to Rachel she was filled with joy and said, "...God hath taken away my reproach..." Gen. 30:23.

It was not by choice that Jacob had two wives but it was because Laban, his father in law cheated him in making Leah, his first daughter to take place of Rachel, his second daughter, through a cunning plot that Leah became the first wife of Joseph, and Rachel became the second.

Jacob is blessed and his name is called as "Israel" by God. He had twelve sons and they are the twelve tribes and she gave birth to her second son, Benjamin. She had her last breath after giving birth to Benjamin. (Gen. 35:16-20).

Jacob loved Rachel, more than he did love Leah, and, therefore, he loved Jacob and Benjamin more than he did love his other children through Leah.

From turbulent days when he was sold in to Egypt for interpreting Jacob's dreams that not only Jacob disliked but all other brothers also disliked, to the times when he became a great ruler in Egypt, his life journey was very interesting one.

He faced what appeared as insurmountable problems of being sold in to Egypt, put in Jail, on false charges of molestation, which he never attempted, to the times when he had to take up an important assignment of managing the situation during famine, his life events bring in us new thoughts as to how God will be with his children.

Joseph had a humble beginning and suffered troubles and trials; nevertheless, God was with him always. He surrendered himself to the will of God, and, therefore, had a successful life in the end.

God led him from a humble life to an important place. Later in his life, Joseph was restored to his honor after being released from prison, and was made a ruler in Egypt. The honor was so great in the land of Egypt was so great that Pharaoh took his ring off his hand and put on Joseph's hand and said...

"...And Pharaoh said unto Joseph, I am Pharaoh, and without thee shall no man lift up his hand or foot in all the land of Egypt." Genesis 41:44

Not only Pharaoh honored Joseph, who was of the age of 30 years, with great power in the land of Egypt but he also gave him "Asenath" the daughter of Potipherah priest of On.

Joseph visited entire land of Egypt. In the seven-year-period of abundance Joseph gathered up the food and made available in the cities. He gathered corn as the sand of the sea until he stopped counting the number of them.

Joseph was blessed with two sons by Asenath and they were born before the famine came upon. Joseph called the firstborn as "Manasseh" and the second one as "Ephraim".

In remembrance of his ability to forget his entire toil and troubles Joseph named first one as Manessah and in remembrance of his prosperity in the land of affliction he named the second one as Ephraim.

As God revealed earlier to Joseph through the dreams famine came upon all the lands but in the land of Egypt there was bread.

During that severe famine people cried to Pharaoh for help and he ordered that they may go to Joseph. Joseph opened the barns for selling the food and the people of all countries went to him to buy food. (cf. Genesis 41:46- 57).

CHAPTER 13

HOLY SPIRIT CONVICTS OF

1. SIN
2. RIGHTEOUSNESS
3. JUDGMENT

THE SPIRIT OF LORD JESUS CHRIST

Lord Jesus Christ said after He has gone to the Father, Holy Spirit will come into this world and will help His disciples with teaching of all things and bringing to our remembrance all that He said to them. The disciples did not understand, until after His resurrection from the dead, many things the Lord said to them while He was on this earth calling for repentance, performing miracles, and healing the sick etc.

After forty days of His staying in this world after resurrection in order to show Himself that He has risen from the dead, the Lord ascended into heaven. He is now seated at the right hand of the Father and pleading on our behalf. While the Lord is in heaven, His Spirit is in our hearts guiding us, comforting us, teaching us the things of God.

Holy Spirit is living person, and, therefore, we do not refer Holy Spirit as "it", but we refer Holy Spirit as "Him". While the Lord Jesus Christ is pleading on our behalf with the Father all the time, His Spirit is in us comforting us, and guiding us.

"Consequently, he is able to save to the uttermost those who draw near to God through him, since he always lives to make intercession for them" – Hebrews 7:25 ESV

"If then you have been raised with Christ, seek the things that are above, where Christ is, seated at the right hand of God" – Colossians 3:1 ESV

The Lord said He will be with us forever providing us heavenly peace, the peace that transcends every understanding. His Spirit is always with us and is in us.

God is Triune; the Father, the Son, and the Holy Spirit. They are not three Gods, but One God in three. Their functions are different, yet they are one.

Anyone understanding Holy Spirit as a different entity other than the Spirit of Lord Jesus Christ, gets into trouble of misunderstanding and misinterpreting Scriptures. Those, who misunderstand Scriptures and misinterpreting them go further accusing Christians, who do not behave in a peculiar way of worshipping that they do not have Holy Spirit in them.

When an unbeliever accepts Lord Jesus Christ as his/her savior, He instantly comes into his/her heart. That is to say His Spirit instantly enters and lives in his/her heart.

"For God so loved the world, that he gave his only Son, that whoever believes in him should not perish but have eternal life" – John 3:16 ESV

"Have this mind among yourselves, which is yours in Christ Jesus, who, though he was in the form of God, did not count equality with God a thing to be grasped, but emptied himself, by taking the form of a servant, being born in the likeness of men. And being found in human form, he humbled himself by becoming obedient to the point of death, even death on a cross. Therefore God has highly exalted him and bestowed on him the name that is above every name, so that at the name of Jesus every knee should bow, in heaven and on earth and under the earth, and every tongue confess that Jesus Christ is Lord, to the glory of God the Father" – Philippians 2:5-11 ESV

"But the Helper, the Holy Spirit, whom the Father will send in my name, he will teach you all things and bring to your remembrance all that I have said to you" – John 14:26 ESV

We are sealed with the Promise of the Holy Spirit after we have heard the word of truth, the Gospel of salvation, and believed in Lord Jesus Christ, who gave His Spirit in our hearts as a guarantee. He said, "…I will never leave you nor forsake you." – (cf. 2 Corinthians 1:22; Ephesians 1:13; Hebrews 13:5 ESV)

Holy Spirit never enters the heart of an unbeliever. However, He starts convicting unbeliever as soon as the unbeliever starts responding to the preaching of the Gospel. Thus, He reproves him/her of sin, and of righteousness and of judgment. God gave apostles, prophets, evangelists, pastors and teachers to preach, teach the Word of God, and baptize those who accept Lord Jesus Christ as their personal savior (Ephesians 4:11).

Immediately an unbeliever accepts Jesus as Lord and confesses his/her sins to the Lord, and believes in heart that God raised Him from the dead on the third day, he/she is saved and assured of everlasting life, and sealed with the earnest of the Spirit in their hearts (cf. 2 Corinthians 1:22).

Does Holy Spirit do the work directly, independently, secretly – NO! The conversion is always by preaching, and the listener hearing the word, and by believing in the Word of God. Holy Spirit by means of WORD convicts, paves the way for conversion, and indwells heart.

"So then faith cometh by hearing, and hearing by the word of God" (Romans 10:17)

The Lord opens the heart through the preaching of the Gospel. Those who hear the Word of God, believe and obey. When you hear the Gospel of Jesus Christ, it pricks the heart. Holy Spirit shows you the Truth. That is how Holy Spirit convicts of sin, righteousness, and judgment. He does not do anything by stealth, or independently and never directly. Holy Spirit never convicts anyone of sin, righteousness, and judgment where there is no preaching done, or some reading material relating to Gospel of Jesus Christ is not provided.

Once, Holy Spirit indwells the heart of the saved one, the action is irreversible. It is immediate and it is God's act. The believer in Christ does not need to wait for Holy Spirit to indwell him/her. The indwelling of Holy Spirit is not an action by man, but is it the act of God.

"Now when they heard this, they were pricked in their heart, and said unto Peter and to the rest of the apostles, Men and brethren, what shall we do?" (Acts 2:37)

Acts 16:14-15 – Paul preached. Lydia heard the Gospel of Jesus Christ and believed in Jesus Christ.

Acts 18:1-8 – Paul preached, Crispus believed and obeyed the WORD of God.

There are many more examples.

The following is a response to a question whether Jesus preached stealthily and would Holy Spirit work stealthily or not.

The word "Stealth" is a derivative of "steal". Definition of stealth according Webster's dictionary:

STEALTH (n)

The act of stealing; theft. The owner proves the stealth to have been committed on him by such an outlaw.

The thing stolen

Secret act; clandestine practice

The act or action of proceeding furtively, secretly, or imperceptibly

Did Jesus preach going like a thief? No, Never! Did He promote preaching like a thief steals something? No, Never! In fact, Jesus did very few miracles and very less ministry in His hometown, Nazareth. It is because they rejected Him, and did not believe in Him.

References:

"And they were offended in him. But Jesus said unto them, A prophet is not without honour, save in his own country, and in his own house. And he did not many mighty works there because of their unbelief" (Matthew 13:57-58)

"For Jesus himself testified, that a prophet hath no honour in his own country. Then when he was come into Galilee, the Galileans received him, having seen all the things that he did at Jerusalem at the feast: for they also went unto the feast" (John 4:44-45)

Read view of Nathaniel, who was also called as "Bartholomew" about Nazareth…

"Philip finds Nathanael, and says unto him, we have found him, of whom Moses in the law, and the prophets, did write, Jesus of Nazareth, the son of Joseph. And Nathanael said unto him, Can there any good thing come out of Nazareth? Philip saith unto him, Come and see. (John 1:45-46)

DID JESUS PREVENT PREACHING AT ANY TIME?

Yes; but does that violate "Great Commission" in Matthew 28:19-20. No! God has His priorities. In Matthew 10 we see

Jesus prohibiting His disciples to go into the way of the Gentiles and into any city of Samaritans.

These twelve Jesus sent forth, and commanded them, saying, Go not into the way of the Gentiles, and into any city of the Samaritans enter ye not: (Matthew 10:5)

He said...

"And whosoever shall not receive you, nor hear your words, when ye depart out of that house or city, shake off the dust of your feet. Verily I say unto you, It shall be more tolerable for the land of Sodom and Gomorrah in the Day of Judgment, than for that city" (Matthew 10:14-15)

"Now when they had gone throughout Phrygia and the region of Galatia, and were forbidden of the Holy Ghost to preach the word in Asia" (Acts 16:6)

However, in due course of time, in a different dispensation, Jews and Gentiles are made "one New Man" "That the Gentiles should be fellow-heirs, and of the same body, and partakers of his promise in Christ by the gospel" (Ephesians 3:6)

It is not that certain country, or continent, or area on the earth is cut out from salvation by God, but it is a matter of priorities set by God.

"For I am not ashamed of the gospel, for it is the power of God for salvation to everyone who believes, to the Jew first and also to the Greek" Romans 1:16

CHAPTER 14

REPENTANCE AND CHRISTIANITY

It is interesting to note that Lord Jesus never said about conversion from one's religion to Christianity; but rather what He said was to "Repent".

In the normal course of reading Bible we do not need to consider how a certain word was used in the original language, but when it becomes contentious, it is necessary that we search the actual meaning of that word used in a given context, and it is imperative that we understand correctly as to how the said word was used in the language in which it was originally written.

The title "Christians" for the followers of Christ has come into existence much later after Jesus died and rose from the dead, and ascended into heaven. The title "Christians" was given in derision by the enemies of followers of Christ, as some believe. Reading through Acts chapter 11 would give good idea as to why the followers of Christ were called "Christians".

"And when he had found him, he brought him unto Antioch. And it came to pass, that a whole year they assembled themselves with the church, and taught much people. And the disciples were called Christians first in Antioch" (Acts 11:26)

"Yet if any man suffer as a Christian, let him not be ashamed; but let him glorify God on this behalf" (1 Peter 4:16)

FEW LINES FROM HISTORY

King Saul, King David and King Solomon ruled whole of Israel, but King Saul's ways were not pleasing to God, and, therefore, the LORD gave the reign to King David, who was successful for many years, but on one point he failed. He counted his army as if to show that he was winning wars by his own power. In fact, he won all his wars with the help and leadership of God.

When it was time for David's son, Solomon to take over the reign the LORD gave him David's throne and said to him to keep the LORD's commandments and statutes.

King Solomon, however, disobeyed God and married wives from heathen, who led him to worship idols. His disobedience resulted in God's wrath coming upon him. God split his kingdom into two; giving northern kingdom to Jeroboam, and the southern kingdom to Rehoboam.

Nineteen kings ruled northern kingdom in succession, and twenty kings ruled southern kingdom in succession. Thereafter, Babylonians under the leadership of Nebuchadnezzar took over Southern Kingdom, and Assyrians took over Northern Kingdom. Finally Babylonians humbled Assyrians, and the history is huge thereafter.

When Jesus came into this world, His initial mission was to the Jews, and then to the Gentiles. He said

"...Repent ye: for the kingdom of heaven is at hand" (Matthew 3:2)

He was in fact saying to them, the united kingdom of Israel was soon to come, and they should change their understanding about Jesus, who repeatedly said to them He came from the Father, making it clear that He was the Messiah.

However, Jews rejected Him as Messiah, which resulted in postponing uniting Northern Kingdom and Southern Kingdom and making them one. Jews expected Messiah to come like a king and like a warrior and defeat opposing forces, and establish earthly kingdom uniting Northern Kingdom and Southern Kingdom.

However, the Lord came into this world in a humble way. He relinquished His glory with the Father, and incarnated in the form of a servant and in the likeness of man. He was born of Virgin Mary, when the Holy Spirit came upon her and the power of the High overshadowed her.

Therefore, He was called the "Son of God". Mary wrapped Him in swaddling clothes, and laid in a manger because there was no room for them in the inn (cf. Luke 1:35; Luke 2:7)

The Lord's second coming of Lord Jesus Christ is imminent. The Lord will "descend from heaven with a shout, with the voice of the archangel, and with the trump of God: and the dead in Christ shall rise first: Then we which are alive and remain shall be caught up together with them in the clouds, to meet the Lord in the air: and so shall we ever be with the Lord" (1 Thessalonians 4:16-17)

"In a moment, in the twinkling of an eye, at the last trump: for the trumpet shall sound, and the dead shall be raised incorruptible, and we shall be changed" (1 Corinthians 15:52)

After the Lord makes His second appearance on this earth, He will literally rule for thousand years from the throne of David in due course of time. The prophecies will literally be fulfilled.

People who saw Jesus perform miracles were in hurry to make Him King, rather than wait for the Lord's time. They were impressed by His ministry.

Therefore, at one point of time they tried to take Jesus by force and make Him King over Israel, but the Lord refused such invitation, and left them. His hour had not come. He will be King of kings, and Lord of lords surely when the Father enforces His time upon men.

"Then those men, when they had seen the miracle that Jesus did, said, this is of a truth that prophet that should come into the world. When Jesus therefore perceived that they would come and take him by force, to make him a king, he departed again into a mountain himself alone" (John 6:14-15)

At the end of His mission, when the Lord was under trial before Pilate, He said His kingdom was not of this world, indicating that His kingdom is of Spiritual kingdom.

"Jesus answered, "My kingdom is not of this world. If my kingdom were of this world, my servants would have been fighting, that I might not be delivered over to the Jews. But my kingdom is not from the world."

Then Pilate said to him, "So you are a king?" Jesus answered, "You say that I am a king. For this purpose I was born and for this purpose I have come into the world—to bear witness to the truth. Everyone who is of the truth listens to my voice." (John 18:36, 37 ESV)

REPENTANCE:

Here, considering how the word "Repent" came into be used, in the context where it was used, it can be seen that the word was translated from the word "metanoeo" from Greek Strong's word 3340 "metanoeo". It means "to think differently or afterwards, i.e. reconsider (morally, feel compunction); not to miss the mark; not transgressing the law".

Hebrew Strong's number: 2398. chata' which means not to miss; it is same as the meaning of 'sin' is. That is not to miss the mark; not transgressing of the law.

Repentance, therefore, is the expression of true sorrow exercised towards God. It is not earning salvation by doing good works. Salvation is by grace through faith and by faith in Jesus Christ alone.

It is the confession one makes of his one's sin committed against the Holy God, and eventually turning away from it altogether. In the context of New Testament it is change one's mind, especially toward Lord Jesus Christ (cf. Luke 3:8-14; Acts 3:19; Acts 26:20).

It is not like a prisoner feeling sorrow after committing a crime. Prisoner might feel sorrow and yet may not change his behavior and attitude; but it is the true sorrow exercised towards the Holy God, and changing altogether his behavior, attitude and life style.

Repentance is just as King David said in his Psalm 51:4.

"Against you, you only, have I sinned and done what is evil in your sight, so that you may be justified in your words and blameless in your judgment" (Psalm 51:4 ESV)

Apostle Paul describes true repentance in 2 Corinthians 7:10 that leads man to salvation; change one's mind that results in abstinence of sinning anymore. He also describes the sorrow of the world that leads to one's death, which consequently leads into the 'lake of fire', where gnashing of teeth does not cease and thirst that never quenches.

"For godly grief produces a repentance that leads to salvation without regret, whereas worldly grief produces death" (2 Corinthians 7:10 ESV)

The following are few references where Greek word "metanoeo" was used in the New Testament, and the corresponding Hebrew word Strong's number 2398 " chata" used in the Old Testament to emphasize on "to think differently or afterwards, i.e. reconsider (morally, feel compunction)"

References: Mt 3:2; 4:17; Mr. 1:15; 6:12; Lu 13:3,5; 16:30; 17:3-4; Ac 2:38; 3:19; 8:22; 17:30; 26:20; 2Co 7:8; Heb. 7:21; Re 2:5,16,21-22; 3:3,19

WHAT DID JESUS MEAN WHEN HE SAID "REPENT"?

Lord Jesus said

"...Repent ye: for the kingdom of heaven is at hand" (Matthew 3:2)

"And saying, the time is fulfilled, and the kingdom of God is at hand: repent ye, and believe the gospel" (Mark 1:15)

"And they went out, and preached that men should repent" (Mark 6:12)

"And that repentance and remission of sins should be preached in his name among all nations, beginning at Jerusalem" (Luke 24:47)

Some theologians think that the phrases "kingdom of heaven", "kingdom of Christ", and the "kingdom of God" refer to different kingdoms, mostly differentiating between "thousand year reign of Lord Jesus" and eternity; but in fact they all refer to one and only "kingdom of God" as we read in Daniel 7:13-14

"I saw in the night visions, and, behold, one like the Son of man came with the clouds of heaven, and came to the Ancient of days, and they brought him near before him. And there was given him dominion, and glory, and a kingdom, that all people, nations, and languages, should serve him: his dominion is an everlasting dominion, which shall not pass away, and his kingdom that which shall not be destroyed" (Daniel 7:13-14)

Peter, the disciple of Jesus said…"Repent ye therefore, and be converted, that your sins may be blotted out, when the times of refreshing shall come from the presence of the Lord" (Acts 3:19)

Sin leads a man to be cast into eternal hell, into "lake of fire" to be precise; but the gift of God is everlasting life.

When Apostle Paul was facing a trial he as a part of his defense he questioned King Agrippa if he believed in Prophets. Replying quickly to this, King Agrippa said "In a short time would you persuade me to be a Christian?"

"vs. 27 King Agrippa, do you believe the prophets? I know that you believe." vs. 28 And Agrippa said to Paul, "In a short time would you persuade me to be a Christian?" Acts 26:27.28

It is interesting conversation. Let us read this passage as it is in the Bible…

Vs. 24 and as he was saying these things in his defense, Festus said with a loud voice, "Paul, you are out of your mind; your great learning is driving you out of your mind."

Vs. 25 But Paul said, "I am not out of my mind, most excellent Festus, but I am speaking true and rational words.

Vs. 26 for the king knows about these things, and to him I speak boldly. For I am persuaded that none of these things has escaped his notice, for this has not been done in a corner.

Vs. 27 King Agrippa, do you believe the prophets? I know that you believe."

Vs. 28 And Agrippa said to Paul, "In a short time would you persuade me to be a Christian?"

Vs. 29 And Paul said, "Whether short or long, I would to God that not only you but also all who hear me this day might become such as I am—except for these chains." Acts 26:24-29 (ESV)

As Apostle Paul was giving his testimony, Festus accuses Paul saying he is out his mind because of his great learning, but Paul says he was not out of his mind, and was speaking the truth.

In the meanwhile, Paul quickly turns to King Agrippa and appreciates King saying the happenings in those days did not escape king's notice, and the kind was not sitting in a corner either!

After hearing from King Agrippa Paul wished if King and all the people there hear him and become the followers of Lord Jesus Christ. It is worth appreciating Paul's boldness in preaching Gospel even while he was in bonds and facing trial.

The title "Christian" may be important, but what is more important is to become a follower of true teachings of Lord Jesus Christ to be surely blessed and to receive everlasting life.

It is not just following the teachings of the Lord, but accepting him into your life as your personal savior, because there is none, who died to save mankind from perishing unto everlasting life, and there is none, except Jesus Christ, who was raised by God unto everlasting life.

We will also die one day; however, all those who believe in Him will be raised from the dead, conformed to His image and live with Him forever and ever. Others will be condemned and judged at the 'great white throne'.

When they are judged as having transgressed the law of God, they will be cast into the 'lake of fire'.

"...if you confess with your mouth that Jesus is Lord and believe in your heart that God raised him from the dead, you will be saved. 10 For with the heart one believes and is justified, and with the mouth one confesses and is saved" (Romans 10:9-10 ESV)

CHAPTER 15

BLASPHEMY AGAINST THE HOLY SPIRIT

"Wherefore I say unto you, All manner of sin and blasphemy shall be forgiven unto men: but the blasphemy against the Holy Ghost shall not be forgiven unto men" (Matthew 12:31)

Blasphemy against the Holy Spirit is very serious. Lord Jesus said, all manner of blasphemy shall be forgiven unto men; but the blasphemy against the Holy Spirit will not be forgiven unto men.

WHAT THEN IS THE BLASPHEMY AGAINST HOLY SPIRIT?

BLASPHEMY is vilification against God. It is evil speaking and railing of the Holy Spirit. It is attributing the work of Holy Spirit to Devil, and/ or attributing Devil's work to the Holy Spirit.

The Lord Himself explained in plain words what the blasphemy is by citing the healing He just then performed as described in Matthew 12:22-32.

There was a demon possessed man, blind and dumb, who was brought to Him for healing. The Lord healed him and the man spoke and saw. Onlookers and those that brought him for healing were all astonished to see the demon left the man, and the man received his vision and speech. They wondered if Jesus was the Son of David!

When the Pharisees, who were jealous of Jesus, and who tried incessantly to put Him in some trap and catch Him, heard of the miraculous healing of the demon-possessed man, who upon receiving sight and speech, spoke and saw, made a highly scathing attack on the Lord, and attributed the work of the Holy Spirit by Him as that of the devil.

They said it is only by Beelzebub, the prince of demons that Lord Jesus had cast out demons. Lord Jesus perceived very quickly their vicious thoughts and said to them that every kingdom divided against itself will be destroyed; they cause damage to themselves, and none of the cities or houses that divide themselves stand firm in any way, but will surely be destroyed.

The Lord questioned them if such be the case and if Satan divides its own kingdom, how could Satan stand firm, and how will his kingdom endure? The Lord was very vociferous in questioning as to by which power their sons would cast the devils out of men, if Beelzebub, prince of peace divides his kingdom?

Further, He explained that if by the power of Holy Spirit He had cast the demon out from the demon-possessed man, then it is obvious that the kingdom of God has come upon them.

He gave an example saying how someone could enter a strong man's house and capture his assets unless he first binds the strong man of the house. After taking the strong man of the house captive, he would plunder strong man's goods, He said.

The Lord, then gave a warning that whoever is not with Him is against Him; and whoever does not gather the good things that the Lord gives, will scatter even that which he/she has.

It is then that Lord Jesus said to them that every sin and blasphemy will be forgiven of men, but the blasphemy against the Holy Spirit will not be forgiven. He said even speaking against the Lord would be forgiven, but whoever speaks against the Holy Spirit will never be forgiven, either in erstwhile age or in future, which is our age.

Lord Jesus Christ, after His resurrection from the dead, was in this world for forty days and ascended into heaven.

As the Lord promised to His disciples in John 14:26; John 15:26; and John 16:7 that He will pray to the Father to send another comforter to be with them and will be with them and in them forever when they are on this earth, the Holy Spirit came into this world as we read in Acts 2:1-7.

The disciples received the power of the Holy Spirit and continued in their ministry for the expansion of the kingdom of God.

The Spirit of Lord Jesus Christ lives within the hearts of the believers, to comfort them, to guide them, and to convict them of their righteousness in God.

"And when he is come, he will reprove the world of sin, and of righteousness, and of judgment" (John 16:8)

"To declare, I say, at this time his righteousness: that he might be just, and the justifier of him which believeth in Jesus" (Romans 3:26)

"And if Christ be in you, the body is dead because of sin; but the Spirit is life because of righteousness" (Romans 8:10)

Inasmuch as the Spirit of Christ lives within the hearts of believers, the blasphemy of Holy Spirit, in this generation, is applicable only to unbelievers and not to believers.

"Therefore I want you to understand that no one speaking in the Spirit of God ever says "Jesus is accursed!" and no one can say "Jesus is Lord" except in the Holy Spirit" – (1 Corinthians 12:3 ESV)

"There is therefore now no condemnation for those who are in Christ Jesus" – (Romans 8:1 ESV)

Therefore, refusal to accept Lord Jesus Christ as Savior, and refusing to believe that God raised Him from the dead is tantamount to blasphemy against the Holy Spirit, and there of no forgiveness of sins to him and it will result in his name being not found in the 'book of life', and eventually being cast into 'lake of fire', where neither gnashing of teeth will cease nor will the thirst quench.

CHAPTER 18

DO NOT GRIEVE THE HOLY SPIRIT

"And do not grieve the Holy Spirit of God, by whom you were sealed for the day of redemption" (Ephesians 4:30 ESV)

Do not cause Holy Spirit to suffer grief. In other words – do not cause Holy Spirit to be mournful or lament. The very instruction that we should not grieve Holy Spirit is to say that we have the capability to grieve Him, cause Him to be sorrowful or allow Him to lament.

The causative actions of believers in grieving the Holy Spirit shows that Holy Spirit is not an influence, or power or inanimate object to refer Him as "it", but the reference should always be as "He", or "His", or "Him" etc. it also shows that Holy Spirit can be grieved, can be lied to, can be blasphemed, or can be quenched.

The grieving of the Holy Spirit is not applicable to unbelievers, because they do not have Holy Spirit in them. They do have conscience, or evil spirit, but not Holy Spirit. Obviously, Holy Spirit will take low profile, when He is grieved by the believer, waiting for him to revive and come back to God.

Even lying in low profile, the Holy Spirit will comfort the believer, convict Him of righteousness, and bestows confidence in him, teaches him to come back to God, and helps backslider to pray and utter intelligible words to the Lord, seeking forgiveness.

Eventually Holy Spirit helps believer to be restored to lead normal Christian life. We, therefore, should not grieve Holy Spirit.

Ephesians 4:30 in its context is to highlight the requirement of a believer in his new life after being born-again.

Once, believer was in the world following the norms of the world, being in sin, slave to Satan and his activities; but now the believer is saved by the grace of God, when he accepted Lord Jesus Christ as his personal savior, and by believing that God raised Jesus from the dead on the third day after the Lord's crucifixion on his behalf on the cross.

Now he is spiritually born-again; born from above, and therefore, he is a new creation in the Lord. He has no more old nature in him; but new nature.

The new nature of a believer demands that he should not walk as the heathen do. The minds of heathen are darkened in their understanding, separated from Godly life in vanity of their minds.

They are separated from God and Godly life because of their ignorance of the knowledge of the truth. Their rocky heart does not melt down to understand the truth. They refuse to know the truth, and mock at the Word of God.

Their greed for money, power and women blinds their spiritual eyes, and therefore, they never give up sensuality, impurity, adultery, fornication, idolatry, which are abominations to the Lord.

Christ-like behavior is to be pure in heart, forgiving one another, and to know that truth is in the "Son of God", who is Lord Jesus.

The former manner of life and its associations such as corrupt life, deceitful desires, should be given up, and thorough renewal of self in the spirit of minds is needed. Thus, one has to put on new self, possess new nature, completely transformed to live like Christ did. The new nature should include to realization of being created in the likeness of God in true righteousness and holiness, putting away falsehood.

Every believer should speak to one another the truth because the entire flock of believers constitutes the body of Christ, and the Lord is the head of the body.

If at all one gets angry for some valid reasons, it should be borne in mind that such anger should not be allowed to continue; but should be discarded before the sun goes down. If it is allowed to continue there is a possibility of anger turns one to become enemy of the other.

It gives opportunity for the devil to take advantage to drift the believer into the darkness of the world. Salvation of believer is never lost, but the blessings are withheld as long as the believer chooses to continue to lead a life unpleasant to the Lord.

As one body of the Lord we, the believers in Christ, should make it a point that no corrupt talk comes out of our mouths. Every effort should be made to see that the body of Christ is built up and His kingdom expands.

Our endeavors in edifying the Lord's body should fit the occasion. Such efforts would render grace to those who hear the Gospel of Jesus Christ.

While doing such work as is pleasant to the Lord, believers should make it a point to see that the Holy Spirit is not grieved. The Holy Spirit is the one, who sealed our salvation for the day of redemption.

The Scriptures demand from every believer that bitterness, wrath, anger, clamor and slander and malice should be discarded from our lives. As the children of God, and as being given the privilege to call God as "Abba, Father", and to be called as "sons of God", we should be kind to one another, tenderhearted, just as the Lord is, toward us. We must forgive one another, as God in His only Son, Jesus Christ forgave us.

If we keep all these instructions we would be under the perfect influence of the Holy Spirit, who will infuse joy, happiness, boldness in our hearts. He will make sure that we rejoice in the Lord.

When we feel sorrowful, He will bring to us joy, and assure us that we belong to the living God, and will be with His Son, Lord Jesus Christ forever and ever, when the Lord comes again. Otherwise, we will be making the Holy Spirit to grieve.

The Holy Spirit does not command us (the believers), or point out our sin, but will lay in low profile and grieves, when we trespass the commands of God. It is too bad to grieve our helper, our comforter, the Holy Spirit, because we are the children of God, born-again, peculiar people chosen by God, a Royal priesthood.

 On the other hand, if we give preeminence to the Holy Spirit to guide us according to His ways, He takes control of our lives. He leads us in a perfect way beneficial to us and to God.

Lord Jesus Christ gave two great commandments; and all the commandments in the Bible come under the purview of these two commandments. The Lord's commandments are…

"And he said to him, 'You shall love the Lord your God with all your heart and with all your soul and with all your mind. 'This is the great and first commandment.' And a second is like it: You shall love your neighbor as yourself. On these two commandments depend all the Law and the Prophets." (Matthew 22:37-40 ESV)

CHAPTER 16

DO NOT QUENCH THE HOLY SPIRIT

The immediate context wherein 1 Thessalonians 5:19 appears is in the final instructions and benediction that Apostle Paul, Silvanus, and Timotheus gave to the assembly of Thessalonians in their first letter to them.

The overall context wherein this verse appears is in the midst of admonitions they gave about the second coming of Lord Jesus Christ. 1 Thessalonians mainly deals with their hope in the Lord Jesus Christ, and their election by God. Paul writes that the Gospel of Christ was proclaimed to them not only in word, and in much assurance but also in power and in the Holy Spirit.

Most assuring words were in 1 Thessalonians 4:16-17, which read...

"For the Lord himself will descend from heaven with a cry of command, with the voice of an archangel, and with the sound of the trumpet of God. And the dead in Christ will rise first. 17 Then we who are alive, who are left, will be caught up together with them in the clouds to meet the Lord in the air, and so we will always be with the Lord"

Some of them were disappointed over the lack of teaching as to what happens to their relatives and friends, who were already dead. They were in dilemma as to whether or not they will rise from the dead, or resurrections have already past. In 2 Thessalonians Paul deals as to how the coming of the Lord will not happen until the 'man of sin' is revealed.

There are two aspects Paul deals in these two epistles. One, of the Lord's coming surprisingly and another, there will be signs and sure visible happenings before the Lord comes again.

The first one, is the Lord's coming for the believers, who are His body, and the bride, to keep them safe from the great tribulation period, which is primarily assigned for the unbelieving Jews, and to the Gentiles, as well. The second advent of the Lord on this earth is spoken of, by the Lord Himself, in Matthew 24:4-51.

After Paul having dealt with these issues, he along with his co-workers, Silvanus and Timothy, give few general instructions, and then blesses them.

Paul emphasized on respecting and esteeming highly those who are working for the Lord; to be at peace among themselves. He instructs to admonish the idle, to encourage the weak-hearted (with doubtful thoughts) and help them.

He instructs to be patient with all in order to see that no one repays anyone evil for evil, but seek to do good to everyone. His desire is that we all rejoice always as the Lord desired, and to keep praying always in our hearts and to give thanks to God in all circumstances.

It is the will of God in Christ Jesus, and compulsion, that we may not quench the Spirit of God. He says we should not despise the prophecies but to test all teachings and hold fast that which is good, and to abstain from all form of evil (cf. 1 Thess. 5:12-22)

More specifically 1 Thess. 5:16-21 are important to consider while explaining verse 19 which reads, "Do not quench the Spirit"

- Vs.16 Rejoice always,
- Vs.17 Pray without ceasing,

- Vs.18 Give thanks in all circumstances; for this is the will of God in Christ Jesus for you,
- Vs. 9 Do not quench the Spirit,
- Vs.20 Do not despise prophecies,
- Vs.21 But test everything; hold fast what is good,
- Vs.22 Abstain from every form of evil.

Vs.20 admonishes us not to despise the prophecies that are in the Bible; and not those of dreaming of a beautiful refrigerator in a shopping center, buy and say prophecy fulfilled, or say that a couple will have a child next year! Let us be careful to understand that the testimony of Jesus is the spirit of prophecy"

"Then I fell down at his feet to worship him, but he said to me, "You must not do that! I am a fellow servant with you and your brothers who hold to the testimony of Jesus. Worship God." For the testimony of Jesus is the spirit of prophecy" Revelation 19:10

Vs. 21 admonishes us to differentiate truth from false teachings, and accept only the true teachings.
Vs. 22 admonishes us to abstain from every form of evil. We are called unto do good works.

QUENCHINH THE HOLY SPIRIT?

When it comes to dealing with the specific instruction of not quenching the Holy Spirit, Bible teaches us that unless we give freedom to the Holy Spirit to lead us in accordance with the will of God, we will not grow in Spirit and will not be useful, not only for the service of the Lord, but also will not be useful for ourselves in true growth in Spirit of the Lord.

The ministry of the Holy Spirit in us is identified as "Fire" (cf. Acts 2:2-4). The quenching is to pour water on the fire in order to diminish the effect of fire, or fully extinguish the fire. It means shutting down the power of the Holy Spirit in us to do any good work.

It is so amazing that God, who created the heavens and the earth, and all that is in it, and who sent His one and only Son, Lord Jesus Christ into this world to bear our sin upon Him lives in the form of His Spirit in the tiny heart of the saved man. The LORD declared...

"Thus saith the LORD, The heaven is my throne, and the earth is my footstool: where is the house that ye build unto me? And where is the place of my rest?" (Isaiah 66:1)

"Then Solomon stood before the altar of the Lord in the presence of all the assembly of Israel and spread out his hands toward heaven, 23 and said, 'O Lord, God of Israel, there is no God like you, in heaven above or on earth beneath, keeping covenant and showing steadfast love to your servants who walk before you with all their heart' "(1 Kings 8:22-23 ESV)

Stephen testified of the living God saying the LORD's own words...

"Heaven is my throne, and earth is my footstool: what house will ye build me? Saith the Lord: or what is the place of my rest?"(Acts 7:49)

Although the LORD's Majesty, strength and power are inexplicable by us, yet it is so comforting to us that His Spirit is in our hearts. The Holy Spirit does not forcibly command us to take control of our the desires of our heart, but will keep convicting us of our righteousness of God in Christ, and to pursue comforting us, and helping us to pray to God to return to the LORD.

The very instruction that we should not quench the Holy Spirit shows that man has the capability of refusing to yield to the power of God that is in our hearts by the indwelling presence of Holy Spirit, and refuse to accept His guidance, His comfort, and His conviction of our righteousness in Christ.

Our (believers) bodies, in each case is a temple of God, who dwells by His Spirit in us and, therefore, the said temple is not for defilement, but are to be used for glorifying God, lest otherwise, we would be involving God in our defilement.

Lord Jesus Christ became sin for us once and for all and was condemned on the cross in order that we, by believing Him, as our savior, having become the children of God. Repetition of sins by us causes God to leave us to suffer damage, loss or sickness to our physical bodies.

Nonetheless, our salvation is not lost, but the blessings are lost until we make efforts to restore ourselves unto God and His statutes. Two points here would illustrate how a believer would quickly backslide, and yet there are opportunities available for him to return to the Lord.

When Jesus spoke the truth that "it is the spirit that gives life, the flesh profits nothing: the words that I speak unto you, they are spirit, and they are life" many followers of Jesus left Him.

Then Jesus asked His disciples if they would also go away. Simon Peter, one of His disciples, who took the lead answered Him and said "...Lord, to whom shall we go? You have the words of eternal life". Jesus is the bread of life. All those, who eat of that bread will live forever. (cf. John 6:35)

"I am the living bread which came down from heaven: if any man eat of this bread, he shall live forever: and the bread that I will give is my flesh, which I will give for the life of the world" (John 6:51)

It is, therefore, incumbent upon us that we allow Holy Spirit to work in us, and not quench His work in us (cf. John 6:68)

In another incidence we see an unclean spirit is gone out of a man and wanders and seeks rest in dry places; but finds none. The evil spirit, then goes back to the place where he came from, and sees that the place is empty; good for occupation, neat and clean, well swept and well garnished.

The evil spirit takes advantage of the man, who did not do well to allow Holy Spirit to help him keep his mind engaged in good thoughts, goes and finds seven other wicked spirits more harmful than himself, and forces their entry into the empty heart of the believer. Thus the last stage of the believer becomes worse than the first (cf. Matthew 12:43-45).

God did not allow His Spirit to live in us for resorting to uncleanness, but unto holiness. If anyone despises the truth and quenches the Holy Spirit, he is not despising man, but God. (cf. 1 Thessalonians 4:7-8)

Apostle Paul writes...

"Do you not know that your bodies are members of Christ? Shall I then take the members of Christ and make them members of a prostitute? Never! Or do you not know that he who is joined to a prostitute becomes one body with her? For, as it is written, "The two will become one flesh."

But he who is joined to the Lord becomes one spirit with him. Flee from sexual immorality. Every other sin a person commits is outside the body, but the sexually immoral person sins against his own body. Or do you not know that your body is a temple of the Holy Spirit within you, whom you have from God? You are not your own" (1 Cor. 6:15-19)

"What agreement has the temple of God with idols? For we are the temple of the living God; as God said, 'I will make my dwelling among them and walk among them, and I will be their God, and they shall be my people'" (2 Corinthians 6:16 ESV)

Paul takes pride in testifying about Thessalonians, who made him and his co-workers, to have hope in the Lord and rejoice in Him. He feels his crown of boasting before Lord Jesus Christ would be their obedience to Christ. (cf. 1 Thessalonians 2:19)

He wishes that the Father and the Son may direct the Lord's ways unto us that they may increase and "to abound in the love to one another, and to all even as we also to you, to the establishing your hearts blameless in sanctification before our God and Father, in the presence of our Lord Jesus Christ with all His saints" (cf. 1 Thessalonians 3:11-13 ESV)

CHAPTER 17

WHEN GOD TAKES CARE OF US...

"Come unto me, all ye that labour and are heavy laden, and I will give you rest" (Matthew 11:28)

Jews groaned over ceremonial laws and traditions (cf. Acts 15:10). Lord Jesus tells them to come to Him and to embrace His teachings. He was addressing ruined sinners burdened with consciousness of their transgressions. He calls them to come to Him and trust Him for salvation.

There is redemption for everyone who confess their sins to Him, confess that He is the Lord and believes in heart that God raised Him from the dead.

Everyone, who feels burdened with a situation beyond one's capacity to handle it, will find rest in the Lord, when He takes care of it. All that one has to do is to surrender his problems to God and obey His instructions.

A case in point from Old Testament is of Joseph, who, although struggled many years of his early life, yet in God's time he became a ruler in Egypt.

From his turbulent days to his exalted positon Joseph witnessed God's immense care and providence for not only his life, but all of his brothers and father (his mother died at Hebron [Gen.23:2] before his father and children entered Egypt).

Joseph was sold into Egypt by his brothers as they envied his interpretations of dreams which foretold that they all will serve him. He faced what seemed to be insurmountable obstacles in his life. He was put in jail on false charges of molesting

Potiphar's wife, while the fact was that she enticed him into sin, but he, being righteous and a follower of God, ran from it (Gen. 39:7-20).

God was with Joseph and helped him to become ruler over the entire Egypt (Gen.41:39-43).

"And he made him to ride in the second chariot which he had; and they cried before him, Bow the knee: and he made him ruler over all the land of Egypt". (Genesis 41:43)

"And Pharaoh said unto Joseph, I am Pharaoh, and without thee shall no man lift up his hand or foot in all the land of Egypt". (Genesis 41:44)

CHAPTER 18

BY THE MIGHTY ARM OF THE LORD

"And the LORD brought us forth out of Egypt with a mighty hand, and with an outstretched arm, and with great terribleness, and with signs, and with wonders" (Deuteronomy 26:8)

Recounting the method God used in order to get the children of Israel out from slavery in Egypt, God's servant Moses speaks to them and admonishes them not to forget God's help rendered to them in the past.

It was just before they occupied the land of Canaan the Promised Land that Moses speaks to them saying the Land is given to them, and they need to go with confidence and possess it and live therein. He says to them that, as a token of thanksgiving, they should take of the first of all the fruit of the earth and bring to the LORD.

The LORD says that they should acknowledge God's help without which they would never have entered into the Promised Land. The LORD swore to their fathers that He will give unto them the Promised Land flowing with milk and honey, and He gave it to them. The priest should then take the offering and set it before the altar of the LORD.

It was again confessing time for them. They should say that Jacob, their father, whom they call as Syrian (one, who led a nomad life), went down into the land of Egypt, and "sojourned there with a few, and became a nation, great, mighty, and populous".

Egyptians took advantage of them and burdened them with slavery, and afflicted them terribly. The LORD God heard their voice and took pity on them. He saw their affliction, their hard labor, and suffering were unbearable and they were under great oppression.

The LORD, therefore, brought them out of Egypt with His mighty hand, and with an outstretched arm. He led them in the wilderness. He provided them food and water, and finally gave them the Canaan, the blessed Promised Land flowing with milk and honey.

It was God's command that they should acknowledge God's help and guidance. They were required to say that they brought their first-fruits of the land, which the LORD gave them. They were require to set offering before them and worship Him (cf. Deut. 26:1-10)

The LORD who helped the children of Israel get out of the slavery, sent His one and only Son into this world that whoever believes in Him shall not perish but will have everlasting life.

Lord Jesus Christ is the Good shepherd, who feeds His flock and will gather His sheep with His mighty and outstretched arm. He carries them in His bosom, and gently leads those that are with young.

"He shall feed his flock like a shepherd: he shall gather the lambs with his arm, and carry them in his bosom, and shall gently lead those that are with young". (Isaiah 40:11)

As a Good Shepherd the Lord walks slowly along with the sheep at their pace, and guards the herd in the barn waiting at its doorway. He is the keeper and He is the door. Neither any thief, nor any wolf can enter sheep barn unless the enemy first encounters the Shepherd, and if such thing happens, the Good Shepherd's outstretched arm will prevail over the enemy. He is our Lord and He is our Almighty God. His mighty and outstretched hands help us in our troubles and trials. He protects us from all peril.

He says no one can come to the Father but by Him.

"Jesus said to him, 'I am the way, and the truth, and the life. No one comes to the Father except through me' ". (John 14:6)

Prophet Isaiah prophesied seven hundred years before Jesus came into this world that the Lord is Almighty one, who will His Government over all the powers, governments, and the people of the world.   He is the Son of God, the incarnate God, the very image of the invisible God, who came in the likeness of man and lived among us. Jesus asserted that the Father and He are one.

Almighty God, our Lord has His mighty arms outstretched always inviting us to have fellowship with Him. Who can measure His mighty power? Who can fathom His love for us? Who can understand His ways? Prophet Isaiah says about the Lord thus...

"Who hath measured the waters in the hollow of his hand, and meted out heaven with the span, and comprehended the dust of the earth in a measure, and weighed the mountains in scales, and the hills in a balance? Who hath directed the Spirit of the LORD, or being his counsellor hath taught him? With whom took he counsel, and who instructed him, and taught him in the path of judgment, and taught him knowledge, and shewed to him the way of understanding?" (Isaiah 40:12-14)

"For my thoughts are not your thoughts, neither are your ways my ways, saith the LORD" (Isaiah 55:8)

CHAPTER 19

PASS THE GOOD NEWS ON

"In whom ye also trusted, after that ye heard the word of truth, the gospel of your salvation: in whom also after that ye believed, ye were sealed with that Holy Spirit of promise" (Ephesians 1:13)

We received salvation by grace through faith in Lord Jesus Christ and Him alone. Therefore, it is incumbent upon us to be grateful to the Lord for His sacrifice for us, and dying a substitutionary death on the cross of Calvary on behalf of us.

We find solace in Him, who promised us that we will not only see Him face to face when He comes again, but we will be conformed to His image, and will be with Him forever and ever. It is a promise made by God that we are sealed with the Holy Spirit of promise.

A Lamb by each household of the children of Israel, was slain by the children of Israel, and its blood was applied to the lintel posts of each of their homes in order to escape from the wrath of the LORD against the Egyptians, who held them as slaves for four hundred years. The LORD killed all the first born of the Egyptians and their cattle, while saving all the first born of the Israelites.

The Lord redeemed us from the bondage of sin, and therefore, we should be thankful to Him more than anything that we have. We are thankful to the Lord for writing our names in the "book of life".

Our desire is that those, who have not known the goodness of Lord Jesus Christ, may come to know His love for mankind, and the salvation that He offers. Not for any earthly riches that we strive for, but for heavenly inheritance that the Lord promised to us that we strive for. Our rewards are in heaven. Lord Jesus said...

"But seek ye first the kingdom of God, and his righteousness; and all these things shall be added unto you". Matthew 6:33

Just as the children of Israel suffered bondage of slavery under Pharaoh in Egypt, we were also held captive under Satan. Just as the children were redeemed from the bondage of slavery, we are also redeemed from the bondage of slavery under sin.

The LORD led the children of Israel and helped them cross the Red Sea, which He parted into two to make way for them to tread on the dry pathway all the way to the other side of the shore. Their enemy led by Pharaoh and His mighty warriors, who pursued them from behind, and his chariots were all drowned by the LORD in the Red Sea.

The LORD went before them in a pillar of cloud by day and in a pillar of fire by night. The pillar of cloud and the pillar of fire were always there for their protection. The LORD took of the wheels of their chariots and caused great havoc for Egyptians.

The innocent children of Israel were to do nothing except trust God and follow His commands. It was all by the LORD, and by His mighty power that the enemy was destroyed, granting incredible victory to the children of Israel (cf. Exodus 13:18-22 and 14:24-3).

Speaking to His disciples, Lord Jesus Christ said to them not to be troubled in their hearts, but instead believe in God and believe in Him, as well. He is the Son of God, the very incarnate

God Himself. Jesus Christ is the same yesterday, today and forever.

"Jesus Christ the same yesterday, and today, and forever" (Hebrews 13:8)

"And fear not them which kill the body, but are not able to kill the soul: but rather fear him which is able to destroy both soul and body in hell" (Matthew 10:28)

CHAPTER 20

THE LAST DAYS OF JESUS

In the last section of the Gospel according to Matthew, chapters ranging from 21 to 28 a quick outlook of great achievements of Lord Jesus Christ is seen.

It starts with His triumphal entry into Jerusalem as the King of Jews, followed by the exercise of His authority in the Temple, teachings on the Kingdom of heaven, resurrection, the encounter with hypocrisy of Pharisees, teachings on the Parable of fig tree, the end times, the second coming of Jesus, Sheep and Goat Judgment, salvation to left behind Jews and Gentiles, His praying in Gethsemane before His crucifixion, the betrayal by Judas Iscariot, His trial and crucifixion, resurrection, and His command to His disciples to preach the Gospel.

The day of triumphal entry of Jesus into Jerusalem corroborates with the tenth day of the month Abib, which God designated as the first month for His people, the people of Israel (Ref. Exodus 13:1; 23:15;34:18; Deut. 16:1)

"Observe the month of Abib, and keep the Passover unto the LORD thy God: for in the month of Abib the LORD thy God brought thee forth out of Egypt by night". (Deuteronomy 16:1)

"This month shall be unto you the beginning of months: it shall be the first month of the year to you". (Exodus 12:2)

The name of the month "Abib" was later changed as "Nissan" (cf. Nehemiah 2:1; Esther 3:7).

THE TRIUMPHAL ENTRY OF LORD JESUS

After Jesus had healed two blind men, He and His disciples drew near unto Jerusalem and came to Bethphage, unto the Mount of Olives.

The Lord then sent His two disciples with instructions that they should go into the village opposite to them. There, He said, they will find a donkey tied and a colt with her.

He said that they should unloosen them and bring them to Him, and that, in the meanwhile, if anyone asks them as to why they were taking away the donkey and the colt, they should say that the Lord has need of them, and the man will send them immediately.

It shows great rapport among Jesus and the man, who willingly offered the donkey and the colt to be used by the Jesus.

The lowliness of Lord Jesus Christ exhibited here is incredible and awesome. Apostle Paul exhorts in believers in Ephesus and in Philippi as follows:

"I therefore, the prisoner of the Lord, beseech you that ye walk worthy of the vocation wherewith ye are called, With all lowliness and meekness, with longsuffering, forbearing one another in love" (Ephesians 4:1-2)
"Let nothing be done through strife or vainglory; but in lowliness of mind let each esteem other better than themselves" (Philippians 2:3).

As the Lord commanded His disciples they went and brought the donkey and the colt and, thereafter, they laid their clothes on the donkey and the colt and set Jesus on the donkey.

The Lord sat on the donkey and rode on it. A very great multitude of people spread their garments in the way, while others cut down branches (leaves) from the trees, and spread them in the way, The multitudes, who went before and those who followed cried saying "Hosanna to the son of David: Blessed is he that comes in the name of the Lord: Hosanna in the highest. When the Lord entered into Jerusalem, the entire city was moved and questioned as to who He was! The multitude testified that He was the Jesus, the prophet of Nazareth of Galilee.

The riding on the donkey by Lord Jesus Christ and His triumphal entry into Jerusalem were the fulfillment of Prophecy proclaimed in Isaiah 62:11 and Zechariah 9:9.

"Behold, the LORD has proclaimed unto the ends of the earth, Say you to the daughter of Zion, Behold, your salvation comes; behold, his reward is with him, and his work before him" (Isaiah 62:11)

"Rejoice greatly, O daughter of Zion; shout, O daughter of Jerusalem: behold, your King comes unto you: he is just, and having salvation; lowly, and riding upon a donkey, and upon a colt the foal of a donkey" (Zechariah 9:9)

The shadow of crucifixion of Jesus is seen in Exodus 12:1-51

The children of Israel were instructed to take a lamb without any blemish on the tenth day of the month Abib and set it apart until the fourteenth day of the said month.

Every family has to set apart one lamb each for their house, and if the household is too small for the lamb they can share with the household next to their house according to the eating capacity of the number of persons.

The lamb shall be killed on the fourteenth day of the month and its blood shall be applied to the lintel posts of the house in order that the LORD on the day of Passover may pass the house without killing the firstborn in the house.

The children of Israel were instructed to do this act in order that the LORD may kill all the firstborn of Egyptians, including that of Pharaoh, and redeem the children of Israel from the bondage of slavery.

Pharaoh had refused to release the children of Israel from the bondage of slavery in spite of God bringing upon him and on the land of Egypt nine plagues until then.

The killing of the firstborn of the Egyptians was the result of tenth plague, which was the last and final plague that was brought upon them by the LORD God Jehovah. After facing this dreadful plague Pharaoh released the children of Israel from the bondage of slavery.

This was a shadow of the substance that was to happen in due course of time. It was fulfilled in the life of Jesus, who was set apart by the Father in heaven, to be a propitiation for mankind.

Lord Jesus Christ completed His ministry in surrounding areas of Jerusalem, and when it was time for Him to offer Himself as a sacrifice dying a substitutionary death on behalf of us, He made a triumphal entry into Jerusalem. It was fulfilled according to God's timing.

Sometimes men try to go intervene in God's plan and try to help Almighty God, as if God cannot take care of His plans. John 6:15 records an interesting incidence where it says few men tried to help God by forcibly taking Jesus from the midst of congregation to make Him the King of Jews.

They did it when people were convinced that He was the Messiah after seeing the miracles done by Him. Jesus avoided such an action by them and He went into a mountain alone.

"When Jesus therefore perceived that they would come and take him by force, to make him a king, he departed again into a mountain himself alone" (John 6:15)

He was born king as we read in Matthew 2:2, 11. The wise men fell down and worshipped not Mary, His mother, but Him, and they offered gold, frankincense, and myrrh as gifts.

And when they came into the house, they saw the young child with Mary his mother, and fell down, and worshiped him: and when they had opened their treasures, they presented unto him gifts; gold, and frankincense, and myrrh. (Matthew 2:11)

The prophecy in Revelation 19:16 declares Him as the "...KING OF KINGS, AND LORD OF LORDS" (Revelation 19:16). Revelation 20:1-7 declares that Jesus will reign the whole earth for one thousand years. The crucifixion and second coming of Jesus is prophesied in Zachariah 12:10; 13:1; 14:4 and Romans 11:26-29

On the fourteenth day of the month of Abib, immediately after celebrating Passover, the Lord instituted Lord's Supper to remember Him (ref. Luke 22:15-20)

 "In the fourteenth day of the first month at evening is the LORD's Passover" (Leviticus 23:5)
"And on the fourteenth day of the first month is the Passover of the LORD" (Numbers 28:16)

Luke 22:21-71; Luke 23:1-56 records the sequence of events of crucifixion of Jesus, and Luke 24:1-53 records the resurrection and related events.

Our sin was judged on the cross, and we, who confessed our sins to Him, and confessed Him as Lord, and believed that God raised Him from the dead on the third day after His death, were saved and are promised everlasting life to be with Him forever and ever.

CHAPER 21

JESUS CHRIST IS THE SAVIOR

Why did Jesus come in to the world?

There was story told once that a man was sitting in porch watching birds play in the snow, but when it became unbearable for them to stay any longer in the cool weather outside they sought refuge in to the house, but they feared man sitting in the porch.

The man moved a bit and invited them to come in, but they would not come in. The man threw few grains, yet they would not come in because of the fear that the man might harm them. Then the man thought that he should become one like them and invite them in to the house.

Yes, when he became one like them and invited them, they readily accepted him and hopped in to the house. Similarly, God is so great and awesome that we would not be able approach him unless he became a man to be the mediator for us and lived among us.

The Bible says no man has ever seen God. Moses asked for seeing him, but he could see only the back portion of him, when he walked by the cleft, where God stationed him to watch him pass by.

That is why, the Father in heaven sent his One and only Son in to the world to become one like us and to preach about the Kingdom of God. Jesus told us that He and the Father are one. Jesus lived a poor life and walked great distances on this earth, and also went by small boats to reach places to preach repentance and the imminence of the Kingdom of God.

Jesus did miracles on this earth, healed many sick, freed men from the possession of demons, raised dead and finally He became the perfect sacrifice for us.

God placed Adam and Eve to move freely in the Garden of Eden, and God walked with them in the cool of the day. But one day, Satan went to them and deceived them by asking them to eat the fruit forbidden by God.

Satan said to Eve that if they ate the forbidden fruit, they would become like God and their eyes will be open. The eyes of Adam and Ever were opened not to see God any more but to become sinners. They found that they were naked and ashamed of coming out to see God any more when he called them.

God provided them skin coats and concealed their shame and nakedness. They lost the grace of God and became sinners. Often there is heard among Christians and others as to how someone could die for our sins and we receive Salvation. Their question arises as a consequence of their hearing that Jesus died for our sins and whoever accepts him will be saved.

The Bible provides answer and if anyone seeks answer outside the Bible, he/she is only casting aspersions on the efficacy of the precious blood shed on the cross by the Lamb of God, who did many miracles in his time on the earth and showed the way to salvation.

The Answer we receive from the Holy Scriptures is yes. Apostle Paul writes in epistle to the Romans 3:25 "Whom God hath set forth to be a propitiation through faith in his blood, to declare his righteousness for the remission of sins that are past, through the forbearance of God" and in

Romans 5:12 "Wherefore, as by one man sin entered into the world, and death by sin; and so death passed upon all men, for that all have sinned"

Just as sin is inherited by man from his seminal head, Adam, the remission of the sins is possible by the last Adam, Jesus, who bore our sins upon the cross of Calvary and died for.

Just as Moses made a serpent of brass and put it upon a pole, which was lifted high to be seen by everyone, and whoever saw that brass serpent upon the pole was saved, God lifted high and exhibited His one and Only Son upon the cross, and whoever saw and believed in Jesus was saved and will be saved.

The shadow of Jesus becoming the savior was presented in the Old Testament in Numbers 21:9.

The purpose of Jesus dying upon the cross was to provide a way as salvation for whole mankind that whoso ever believes in him shall not perish but have eternal life.

Romans 3:21-27 "But now the righteousness of God without the law is manifested, being witnessed by the law and the prophets; Even the righteousness of God which is by faith of Jesus Christ unto all and upon all them that believe: for there is no difference: For all have sinned, and come short of the glory of God; Being justified freely by his grace through the redemption that is in Christ Jesus: Whom God hath set forth to be a propitiation through faith in his blood, to declare his righteousness for the remission of sins that are past, through the forbearance of God; To declare, I say, at this time his righteousness: that he might be just, and the justifier of him which believeth in Jesus. Where is boasting then? It is excluded. By what law? Of works? Nay: but by the law of faith"

Jesus was the Son of man on this earth, yet He was divine and the Son of God. Jesus lived a perfect and sinless life and bore our sins and died on the cross. Abraham was ready to sacrifice his son, Isaac, but God provided to him a lamb in place of his son, as a sacrifice.

Hebrews 11:17 "By faith Abraham, when he was tried, offered up Isaac: and he that had received the promises offered up his only begotten son" God tested Abraham by asking him to take his only son Isaac in to the land of Moriah, and offer him as a burnt offering upon the one of the mountains, which God would show to him.

Testing is different from that of temptation. God never tempts anyone but he will test his children to see how firm and true they are in their faith. It is the Satan that brings in temptations.

1 Corinthians 10:13 "No temptation has seized you except what is common to man. And God is faithful; he will not let you be tempted beyond what you can bear. But when you are tempted, he will also provide a way out so that you can stand up under it". Abraham by faith took his son Isaac, who willingly obeyed his father's demand of offering a sacrifice and accompanied him. Isaac did not know that he was to be the sacrifice that Abraham had in his mind, but he obediently followed. At one point Isaac even asked his father, where was the lamb of sacrifice.

Genesis 22:7 "And Isaac spoke unto Abraham his father, and said, my father: and he said, here am I, my son. And he said, behold the fire and the wood: but where is the lamb for a burnt offering? Abraham replied to him that God would provide the sacrifice".

Rightly so, God provided sacrifice when Isaac was bound by Abraham, and was placed upon the wood on the altar.

The angel of the LORD appeared unto Abraham and asked him not to lay hands on Isaac. Abraham looked up and saw a ram that was caught in a thicket by its horns. Abraham took the ram and offered him as sacrifice unto the LORD. The death of Jesus was unique in itself. He came down on to this earth from the heavenly place and died for us in compliance to the plan of salvation God had for us. When the offenders of Jesus beat him and flogged Him He could have called for help from the heavenly Father but He did not seek such help.

When Peter cut off one of the ears of soldiers in defense of their attack on his Jesus, he was asked to keep back his sword and was also admonished that those who lived by the sword would die by the sword.

Jesus also asked him if knew that if Jesus desired the Father in heaven would send an army of angels to defend Him. Yes, the Father in heaven would have sent army of angels to kill all those, who persecuted Him, but if He did that the purpose for which He came in to this world would have been defeated.

When Pilate boasted of himself saying he had power to release Jesus or crucify Him Jesus said that Pilate could have no power against Jesus except if it were given him from above.

Jesus also warned him saying whoever delivers him to be crucified had greater sin. (John 19:10-11) Pilate delivered Jesus to be crucified and who wrote a title and put on the cross.

John 19:19 "And Pilate wrote a title, and had it put it on the cross. And the writing was, JESUS OF NAZARETH THE KING OF THE JEWS"

On the cross Jesus gave up his spirit on his own and commended His spirit into the hands of the Father in heaven. He was numbered among the transgressors and none of his bones was broken fulfilling Old Testament prophecies in Isaiah Chapter 53. One of the ecclesiastical law was that Israelites were asked to keep the LORD's Passover (Leviticus 23:5).

In Exodus 12:3-17 instructions were detailed as to how a lamb without any blemish to be offered as sacrifice unto the LORD and the blood of the Lamb be applied on the door posts of their houses so that When the LORD passes by those homes, he would see the blood of the lamb applied and spare their firstborn. In the New Testament the shadow of the sacrifice of the Lamb of God is fulfilled in the crucifixion of Lord Jesus Christ, who died on the cross and taking his blood to the Father in heaven as a perfect atonement.

Hebrews 11:28. Through faith he kept the Passover, and the sprinkling of blood, lest he that destroyed the firstborn should touch them. Jesus became perfect tabernacle for us not made of man, but becoming a sacrifice, mediator, and a high priest for us.

Hebrews 9:11-14 "But Christ being come an high priest of good things to come, by a greater and more perfect tabernacle, not made with hands, that is to say, not of this building; Neither by the blood of goats and calves, but by his own blood he entered in once into the holy place, having obtained eternal redemption for us. For if the blood of bulls and of goats, and the ashes of a heifer sprinkling the unclean, sanctifies to the purifying of the flesh: How much more shall the blood of Christ, who through the eternal Spirit offered himself without spot to God, purge your conscience from dead works to serve the living God?"

As it began to dawn toward the first week of the day, at the end of Sabbath, Mary Magdalene and other Mary came to the sepulcher, where Jesus was laid to rest, after His crucifixion, and death. There was a great earth quake and the angel of the Lord descended and rolled the stone back and sat upon it.

The angel of the Lord proclaimed good news of the risen Lord Jesus Christ. Matthew 28:5-6 "And the angel answered and said unto the women, Fear not ye: for I know that ye seek Jesus, which was crucified. He is not here: for he is risen, as he said. Come, see the place where the Lord lay.

The writer Hebrews says about the risen Lord Jesus Christ, Hebrews 1:3 "Who being the brightness of his glory, and the express image of his person, and upholding all things by the word of his power, when he had by himself purged our sins, sat down on the right hand of the Majesty on high".

His name alone is glorified.

Dear friend,

Believe in Lord Jesus Christ to have everlasting said. "For God so loved the world that he gave his only begotten Son, that whosoever believeth in him should not perish, but have everlasting life". (John 3:16)

CHAPTER 22

BE FILLED WITH THE HOLY SPIRIT

"18 And do not get drunk with wine, for that is debauchery, but be filled with the Spirit,
19 addressing one another in psalms and hymns and spiritual songs, singing and making melody to the Lord with your heart,
20 giving thanks always and for everything to God the Father in the name of our Lord Jesus Christ" (Ephesians 5:18-20 ESV)

Being filled with the Holy Spirit is intermediate periods of time, when we grieve the Holy Spirit, or quench Him.

The moment we forget to give preeminence to Lord Jesus Christ, the Holy Spirit is grieved and quenched. It is then that our speaking in psalms to one another, singing hymns and spiritual songs, and making melody to the Lord in our hearts and giving thanks to God for everything gets dull and boring.

That is why Paul says we should not get drunk with wine, but be filled with the Holy Spirit to see that we worship the Lord in spirit and in Truth.

The moment a sinner is saved, the Holy Spirit takes His residence in the believer's heart to be with him, and in him always. The Holy Spirit will not depart from the heart of believer, even though He is grieved by the believer's actions, or quenched by His inaction, but He stays in low profile always in the heart, convicting the believer of his righteousness of God in Christ.

God has put His seal on us, after establishing us with Christ, and gave His Spirit in our hearts as a guarantee. We heard the word of truth, and the Gospel of Jesus Christ, and believed in Him.

Therefore, we are sealed with the promise of Holy Spirit, who is the guarantee and inheritance until redemption. (cf. Eph. 1:13-14; 4:30; 2 Cor.1:22; John 14:16)

It is noteworthy how Apostle Paul uses the contrast between two phenomena, namely, drunkenness and being filled with Holy Spirit. He calls drunkenness in no lesser words than 'debauchery'.

It is a disease that in most cases leads to death. We may consider at least three cases where character of drunkenness is depicted in the Bible. Right when the Church was being established in Acts Chapter 2, Holy Spirit descended from heaven and came upon the waiting disciples in Jerusalem.

Lord Jesus Christ promised to the disciples that He would pray the Father to send another comforter to be with, and in them. He said to them not to depart from Jerusalem until the Holy Spirit came upon them. He said to them John the Baptist baptized repentant people with water but they will be baptized with Holy Spirit.

After a conversation with His disciples about the kingdom of God, the coming of which, He said, they should not seek to know, the Lord ascended into heaven.

The Lord said to them that they will receive power when Holy Spirit comes upon them, and thereafter they will be witnesses for Him in Jerusalem, and in Judea and Samaria, and then to the utter most parts of the earth. In obedience with the Lord's command they waited at Jerusalem until the Holy Spirit came upon them.

When the Pentecost was fully come they were all together in one place. Then, "suddenly there came from heaven a sound like a mighty rushing wind, and it filled the entire house where they were sitting. And divided tongues as of fire appeared to them and rested on each one of them. And they were all filled with the Holy Spirit and began to speak in other tongues as the Spirit gave them utterance.

Although they did not know various languages as noted in Acts 2:9-11, yet they all spoke with one another the said languages and they all understood one another. Jews, proselytes, Cretans and Arabians heard them talk in their own languages of the mighty works of God. Amazed of what was happening there they were all perplexed and questioned what those strange things happening would mean. Some others said "They were filled with new wine".

However, Peter, the disciple of Lord Jesus Christ stood and lifted up his voice and said to them that they were not drunk, as they supposed, but it was as prophecies by Joel the prophet. (cf. Acts 1:1-11 and Acts 2:1-28)

It makes it clear that baptism by the Holy Spirit and manifestations of the Holy Spirit are not the results of drunkenness. Further, the instruction given by Gabriel, the angel of the Lord that Elizabeth, Zechariah's wife will bear a son, who should be named as John, and he should not drink wine or strong drink because He will be filled with the Holy Spirit.

"for he will be great before the Lord. And he must not drink wine or strong drink, and he will be filled with the Holy Spirit, even from his mother's womb. (Luke 1:15 ESV)

When Timothy was sick, Paul said (cf. 1 Timothy 5:23) that he may drink little wine for the sake of his stomach and for his frequent ailments.

This suggestion shows that wine could be used to take the benefit of their medicinal values, and not to get drunk. Any quantity of wine or alcohol, over and above the medicinal value is detrimental to health and eventually ends up in great deterioration of health, and may even end up in death.

That is the reason why Paul clearly warns believers that they should not get drunk with wine, which is equivalent to debauchery, but to be filled with the Holy Spirit.

Lord Jesus said to worship God in Sprit and in truth, and each one of us should love the LORD God with all our heart, with all our soul, and with all our mind (cf. Matt.22:37). He also said...

 "But when the Helper comes, whom I will send to you from the Father, the Spirit of truth, who proceeds from the Father, the will bear witness about me. And you also will bear witness, because you have been with me from the beginning" (John 15:26-27 ESV)

""And we have seen and testify that the Father has sent his Son to be the Savior of the world" 1 John 4:14 ESV)

"On the last day of the feast, the great day, Jesus stood up and cried out, "If anyone thirsts, let him come to me and drink. Whoever believes in me, as the Scripture has said, 'Out of his heart will flow rivers of living water.'" Now this he said about the Spirit, whom those who believed in him were to receive, for as yet the Spirit had not been given, because Jesus was not yet glorified" (John 7:37-39 ESV)

Apostle Paul says...

"You, however, are not in the flesh but in the Spirit, if in fact the Spirit of God dwells in you. Anyone who does not have the Spirit of Christ does not belong to him" Romans 8:9 ESV

www.ingramcontent.com/pod-product-compliance
Lightning Source LLC
Chambersburg PA
CBHW061742020426
42331CB00006B/1333